Extraordinary acclaim for

MANFRACTIONS

A SURVIVAL GUIDE FOR A METROSEXUAL WORLD

"When it comes to actin' like a man, these guys wrote the book!"

-Doug Hock

"One of the most important literary works of our time."

-Dwayne Hall

"This book slapped me in the face...and I liked it!"

-Jack Stuart

"Unadulterated Genius!"

-Kurt Neuman

"Man-tastic! ('nuff said)"

-Dave Fuino

1

I0132741

MANFRACTIONS

A SURVIVAL GUIDE FOR A METROSEXUAL WORLD

DOUG DRAKE

SCOTT MAETHNER

DEREK GEESKIE

3

MANFRACTION is a registered trademark of

36 BLUE GEES, LLC

Copyright 2008

WWW.MANFRACTION.COM

ISBN: 978-0-615-35553-5

To Mankind

The opinions and ideas expressed in this book were solely generated by the authors, are meant for entertainment purposes only and do not necessarily reflect the positions of the companies, products or individuals listed in this book.

TABLE OF CONTENTS

ACKNOWLEDGEMENTS

The authors would like to thank the followin' "men" for their ideas and support:

Jon "Gwana" Bender
Corvin "Doc" Connolly
Gail "G" Denton
Troy "Krusty" Endicott
Dave "Archie" Fuino
Ronnie "Chief" Giles
Jeff "Cap" Greenwood
Catie "LS" Hague
Dwayne "Ice" Hall
Doug "Hook" Hock
Mike "M2" Manor
Kurt "Neutron" Neuman
Kevin "KO" O'Meara
Ryan "No Neck" O'Meara
Brian "Keepda" Paeth
Jack "JJ" Stuart
John "Stitch" Thomas

WHAT IT MEANS TO BE A MAN

We wrote this book as a tongue-in-cheek look at today's man. Please don't take it too seriously when you read it. We sure didn't when we wrote it.

There are many ways to describe what it means to be a man. We'd like to share ours. To us a real man treats others the way he would like to be treated – with dignity and respect. He doesn't take his family or friends for granted. He works hard every day to make a difference. He supports his family and friends and he looks out for those who are less fortunate. No real man abuses others and no real man abandons his family and friends.

Now enough with the serious stuff...let's get on to the amusement!

INTRODUCTION

You are about to embark on a journey that will take you into a world you thought you knew. A world of actions and words that will likely call into question the very manhood you thought was secure. Welcome to the world of Manfractions!

So, you think you're a man? You think you've got what it takes? We're about to find out! We're gonna show you just how unmanly we've become. Every minute of every day, we're surrounded by Manfractions...they are everywhere! Whether it's men carryin' a hand-bag or men gettin' their hair styled. These kinds of activities must stop! And it starts with you. The only way to keep these Manfractions from pullin' you down into the depths of wussydom is to know what they are, stop doin' 'em yourself, and call 'em out when you see 'em. That's what this book is all about: callin' out the Manfractions so you can stay strong, stay on top and be a man!

Let's start with the definition of Manfraction. Break the word down. First, you have *man*, defined in the American Heritage Dictionary as "a male human endowed with qualities, such as strength, considered characteristic of manhood."[1] We like that word "manhood." You all know this guy. He's strong, he's virile, he's confident, he's not afraid to take a stand. He works hard and plays hard. He

---

[1] Man. (n.d.). The American Heritage® Dictionary of the English Language, Fourth Edition. Retrieved August 23, 2007 from Dictionary.com website.
http://dictionary.reference.com/browse/man.

watches sports on TV – real sports like boxin' and football (not that sissy European futból either). He scratches when and where he wants to, he smokes cigars, drinks beer and doesn't take crap from anybody. He is self-reliant, rational and always ready. He changes his own oil and owns a firearm. He has his own tool belt and air compressor. He can weld two pieces of metal together. He's the kind of guy we all want to be.

Next you have the word _fraction_, which is short for the word infraction, defined as "the act or an instance of infringing; a violation."[2] Breakin' the rules. Now put them together and you have _Manfraction_: any action taken by a man that might be considered an infringement of manhood. That's right; you've done or said somethin' that makes the others around you question your manhood. You've committed a violation so heinous that your buddies are wonderin' why you're not wearin' a skirt.

You can commit a Manfraction at any time. From the time you get out of bed in the mornin' (wearin' either your boxers or nothin' – anythin' else would be a Manfraction) to the time you go to bed at night (after watchin' a couple of hours of sports highlights). You must be constantly on the lookout for Manfractions. From what you wear to what you eat to what you drive to what you say; these things are all susceptible to the Manfraction. As they used to say on Hill Street Blues, "Hey, let's be careful out there."

---

[2] Infraction. (n.d.). The American Heritage® Dictionary of the English Language, Fourth Edition. Retrieved August 23, 2007 from Dictionary.com website.
http://dictionary.reference.com/browse/infraction

There are a few other important things to say about Manfractions.

First, Manfractions are not always cut-and-dried and are often open to interpretation. In many cases, you have to use your best judgment. This book'll help you develop that judgment. When it comes to Manfractions, it's better to be safe than sorry. In other words, "when in doubt – call it out." There's a whole lot of enforcin' to be done out there and we need your help.

Second, if you're gonna commit a Manfraction you should own up to it. When you're cruisin' down the road at 110 miles per hour, you know you're breakin' the rules, but you're willin' to accept what the man'll bring down on you. Likewise, if your fellow man calls you out for committin' a Manfraction, you need to take it like a man. Either correct your behavior pronto or stand up to it if you believe you're doin' what's right. Be proud of that pink shirt, wear your suspenders if you want to, crank up the show tunes, eat crepes, watch figure skatin'...just be prepared to face the consequences. No whinin' and no quibblin'! If you feel very strongly that somethin' you're doin' should be an acceptable man-practice then you owe it to yourself (and to mankind) to take a stand and take a leadership role in changin' the culture.

There are many examples throughout history when this has happened. We will point out two. In retrospect, these were two giant leaps for mankind! One goes back to the invention of the saddle. It used to be very manly to ride a horse bareback. You would just grab your steed, hop on and away you went. However, at some point in history some guy came up with the idea to put somethin' on that horse to ease the ride. Men at the time resisted this change. They laughed at this attempt to "accessorize the horse." They scoffed at the idea of men needin' extra padding. However, common sense prevailed. Man soon realized the tremendous benefits of the saddle. He could ride longer, he had better leverage for huntin' and for battle. And, with saddle bags, he could store stuff like whiskey, tobacco and his rifle. Good stuff indeed!

Another historical example involves the television remote control. It used to be very manly to get up, walk to the TV and turn the knob. Men would use this opportunity to grunt, stretch, get another beer and scratch. They'd train their kids by havin' them change the channels or adjust the volume. But we all know that men today cannot fathom existin' on this Earth without the power and convenience of the remote control.

A third thing to keep in mind about Manfractions is the fact that there are certain times when a Manfraction can be tolerated. There are three basic clauses that can make Manfractions permissible. Don't get us wrong, you're still committin' a Manfraction, it's just that certain situations will provide refuge. For example:

Makin' Momma Happy Clause
Sometimes it's important to make your wife or girlfriend happy. Sometimes you just gotta do what she wants. Fellas, you know what we're talkin' about -- "If momma

ain't happy, ain't nobody happy." And let's face it guys, we men want to be happy! Any Manfraction committed in the pursuit of momma's happiness is just smart livin'. Still a Manfraction, but, at times, well worth it. Some of you uninitiated may call that "whipped," but we just call it "Brilliant!" Now let's not get carried away here. You cannot abuse this clause. For example, you might say that waxin' your back would help make mamma happy, right? Wrong! God gave you that hairy back for a reason! You never know when it might come in handy. The makin' momma happy clause also applies to makin' your kids happy. Skippin' is a wicked Manfraction, unless of course your cute little daughter is holdin' your hand. Bein' a good Dad is manly, not a Manfraction. You get the picture.

Self-Preservation Clause

Sometimes your survival will require that you commit a Manfraction. If whistlin' a show-tune will keep a lunatic from blowin' your brains out then whistle away. If a madman starts shootin' at your feet and says "dance" then you better dance. In these cases, livin' another day is better than avoidin' the Manfraction. Self-preservation can also apply to matters of your health. For example, it

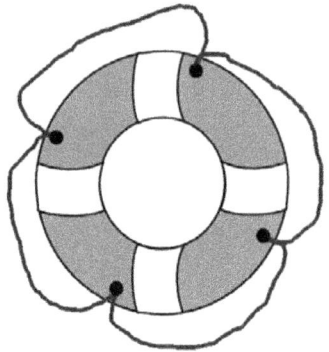

may be acceptable to use lip balm if you are on day-three of a stint in the desert and the blood loss from your cracked lips is addin' to your dehydration. But wait, apply it with your huntin' knife, not from the tube – you never know who may be watchin'.

Acts of Heroism Clause
Under normal circumstances, rippin' off a dude's shirt, lockin' lips with him and holdin' his arm are Manfractions. However, when you're performin' CPR or applyin' direct pressure to stop the bleedin' you get a pass.

Finally, nobody's perfect. No man can live a life without committin' Manfractions. In fact, we can pretty much guarantee that you will not get through this book without realizin' that you've committed at least a few Manfractions.

Before you get any further in this book, we must caution you again...Manfractions are everywhere! Once you read this book, you won't see the world the same way again. That bein' said, let's get started.

CAUTION!
MANFRACTIONS
AHEAD
♂

HOW TO USE THIS BOOK

Know the rules - Live the rules - Enforce the rules

Know the rules, live the rules, enforce the rules. This is the Manfraction MAN-tra. This book doesn't tell you the things to do to be a man. This book tells you the things you and others have to stop doin', pronto, to get your manhood back! Our problem with society today is that there are a lot of men out there (if we can call 'em that) that have started doin' certain things that aren't very manly. This book is also about lettin' others know when they're breakin' the rules. It's about takin' the steps necessary to ensure you and every other man out there know how to act like men.

Consider this book a field guide or a rulebook - a survival guide, if you will, for a *metrosexual* world. Put it in your pocket and take it with you. When you see a potential Manfraction, or think you may have committed one yourself, take out the book and check the rulin'. You may have a pretty good idea already, but the rulebook should set you straight. If the book confirms your gut, call it. Let the dude who broke the rules know what he did. If you are the offender, own up to it. We men have to take care of each other out there. If the suspected action is not in the book, write it in there in the space provided. Then, as soon as you can get to a computer, go to our website (Manfraction.com) and post the Manfraction. Remember, context matters so make sure you tell us all the details. Whenever you post a possible Manfraction, we'll convene the Man Board of Elders to determine a rulin'. If it's a Manfraction we'll officially publish it on Manfraction.com as soon as possible. You can sleep better knowin' you've helped make the world a better place. As soon as we get enough new Manfractions, we'll put out an updated field guide so you and your buddies can be protected. Hey, we're here for you man.

What To Do When You Witness a Manfraction

Enforcin' the rules is vitally important in this day and age. When you see a Manfraction, it is your responsibility to call it out. Point it out to your buddies and those around you. Have the courage to step up and correct strangers. Have the fortitude to stop doin' those questionable things yourself. But, whenever you do this, make sure you use the Manfraction hand signal.

The Manfraction Hand Signal

Not unlike a penalty or foul in sports, Manfractions deserve a hand signal of their own. To signal a Manfraction do the followin': with your hands in close proximity, spread your fingers, and move your hands together and apart several times. There's no need to get excited or give a high-pitched yell (that would be a Manfraction). Just make the hand signal to let those nearby know what's goin' on. A head nod in the general direction of the Manfraction also helps alleviate any ambiguity.

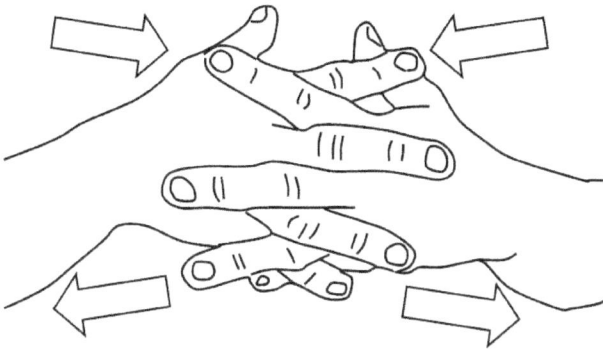

The Manfraction Hand Signal

Man Conditions (MANCONs)

We have discussed how Manfractions are everywhere but the concentration of Manfractions you encounter will vary by time and place. For example, chances are much greater that you will experience more Manfraction activity if your wife drags you to a craft or fabric store than if the two of you went to the stadium to watch your favorite professional football team. To better prepare you to function in and respond to the world around you we've created a warnin' scale to indicate the relative intensity of Manfraction activity. Man Conditions, or MANCONs, establish a baseline understandin' of the Manfraction threat level and help you establish the right mindset before you venture out into the world.

MANCON Normal: A general threat of Manfraction activity exists but warrants only a routine safety and awareness posture. This is a normal day-to-day condition – e.g. drivin' to work. MANCON Normal Measures include: (1) at regular intervals, remind your fellow man to stay strong and to be vigilant; (2) read and re-read this book to enhance your personal readiness.

MANCON Alpha: Minimal threat of Manfraction activity, however, the environment is not predictable. This condition applies when there is a general threat of possible Manfraction activity, the nature and extent of which are unpredictable, and circumstances do not justify full implementation of MANCON Bravo measures. As an example, you're drivin' to work and you hear on the radio that Michael Bolton is havin' a concert in your town that night. Michael Bolton has the potential to draw a crowd inclined to commit Manfractions, but then again, who really is goin' to pay to see this guy? For MANCON Bravo, it may be necessary to implement certain measures from higher MANCONS resultin' from intelligence received or as a deterrent to Manfraction activity. The measures in this MANCON must be capable of bein' maintained indefinitely. MANCON Alpha measures include: (3) Crack your knuckles and limber up your fingers to be ready to call out Manfractions; (4) If you leave home, take this book with you. (5) Be prepared to warn to your fellow man at a moment's   notice.

MANCON Bravo: This condition applies when an increased and more predictable threat of Manfraction activity exists. For example, instead of Michael Bolton, you hear that Elton John is comin' to town. Stay strong because you may have to stay at this posture for weeks on end. Try to minimize hardship to yourself, your family and those around you. MANCON Bravo measures include: (6) avoid the immediate area; (7) warn others of the threat;

(8) voraciously study this book.

MANCON Charlie: This condition applies when an incident occurs or intelligence is received indicatin' some form of Manfraction activity is imminent. As an example, you get wind that your pregnant wife is plannin' on throwin' you a surprise *manshower*. Implementation of measures in this MANCON for more than a short period probably will create hardship and affect day-to-day activities. Measures include: (9) do everything possible to call this off without makin' momma unhappy; (10) If necessary, run away.

MANCON Delta: A Manfraction has occurred or is takin' place, all evasive and/or mitigation procedures should be implemented immediately! This condition applies in the immediate area where a Manfraction has occurred or when intelligence has been received that Manfraction activity is very, very likely. Normally, this MANCON is declared as a localized condition. For example, you're at the Gym in the locker room and a dude bare asses the bench right next to you! Measures include: (11) Call out the Manfraction; (12) evacuate the area ASAP!

The Mantervention
You have to be careful when enforcin' the rules because you never know how people will react. Some men may not take kindly to bein' called out. Some may understand and immediately change their behavior. Some may resist and continue to be in denial, and some may even get violent. For those men you know personally who remain in denial, you should consider holdin' a *Mantervention*. This is a counselin' forum where a group of family

members and close friends gather to confront the dude and offer both support and a plan to change behavior. If at all possible, try to conduct these at manly places like a huntin' lodge or a sports bar. If you are part of a Mantervention, let the perpetrator know you are tired of their actions and then offer your support.

What To Do When You Commit a Manfraction

We're gonna be honest with you. No man can live a life without committin' Manfractions. In fact, we can pretty much guarantee that you will not get through this book without realizin' that you've committed at least a few Manfractions. As you live your life you will, no doubt, commit some more. After all, nobody's perfect. But don't fear, this book will help you through those tough times. There are certain things you can do and certain places you can go to get your manhood back. Refer to the "Absolution" section of this book to see what we're talkin' 'bout.

Men in Trainin'

In addition to helpin' you correct bad behavior, this book is a great learnin' tool for the next generation of men or for those men who've gone astray and are open to gettin' their manhood back. For you fathers, grandfathers and uncles out there, as you learn the rules, please transfer that knowledge to your sons, grandsons and nephews. As you live the rules, please set the example. As you enforce the rules, please take the time to talk to those men in trainin' about why a particular act or deed rose to the level of a Manfraction. It's all about bein' a good MEN-tor. Come to think of it, there is probably not a better graduation gift for young men than this book.

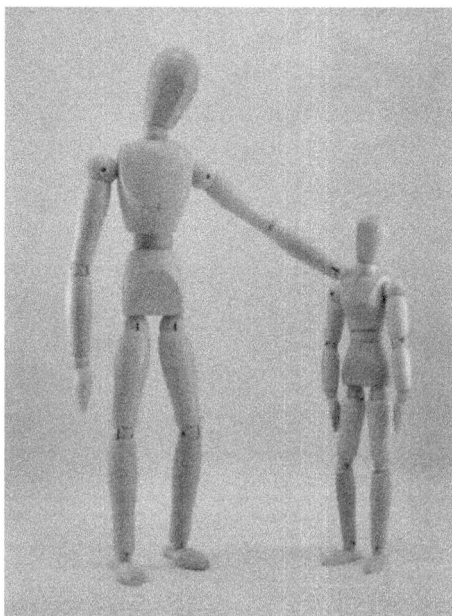

Bein' a good MEN-tor requires knowin' the rules, livin' the rules and enforcin' the rules.

A BRIEF HISTORY OF THE MANFRACTION

Let's face it, the world is becomin' wimpier by the second. Men are drinkin' pink-colored coffees with whipped cream from a straw. They're gettin' facials and their nails done. Some even wear Capri pants. Enough! How did we get to this sorry state? A look back in time and you can clearly see how the male species has gradually given up ground. It's time for us to take back our manhood. <u>Resist</u> modern-day urges to be sensitive, say <u>no</u> if someone offers you fruit in your beer. It will take some time and work but together we can do it. To understand better how we got to our present situation, here is a short look at some Manfractions throughout the ages.

<u>Pre-Historic</u>
Cavemen. Notice how we don't call it cave-people. We don't even acknowledge the cavewoman. Back in the day, it was all about the man! But this era of gruntin' and huntin' wasn't without the Manfraction. Ever since Grog cancelled that outing with the boys to help She-Grog clean the cave, man has started slouchin' toward sissydom.

<u>Middle Ages (4th Century-15th Century)</u>
Mostly, this was a time of the man's man. Knights and warriors roamed the Earth. But these glorious man-times were not entirely Manfraction-free. This is the time in Manfraction history when Anéislis Taylor (that name alone is a Manfraction) first convinced the King to wear silk. Maybe the King thought "he looked nice" or maybe the fabric "felt soft against his skin." Either way the King started a Manfraction that has continued to this day.

Renaissance (14th – 17th Century)

Four centuries of Manfractions. The clothes, the art, you name it. Men in skirts wearin' tights. Men sculptin' naked men out of marble. Michelangelo admittedly had some talent, but he sure was obsessed with naked guys. Sorry Mike, Manfraction!

Age of Enlightenment (18th century)

The age of reason. A good thing. Real men based their decisions on reason, not emotion. We need look no further than MacGyver. Emotion will not help you make a bomb out of bamboo shoots, mud and swamp gas. Overall, this was a pretty good time for the man, but not without a few gaffs. For example, it was durin' this period that a guy named William Herschel discovers a planet...pretty cool, right? Kinda manly. But, then he goes and names it Uranus! What was he thinkin'!? Wait; guess we know what he was thinkin'!

Victorian Age (1837 – 1901)

An era named after the Queen...'nuff said! Powdered wigs and harpsichords. Knickers and ruffled collars. 64 years of Manfractions. Give us a break!

Industrial Age (Late 18th – Early 20th Century)

Very manly times, indeed. Lots of fire, hot coals, forgin' steel, smog, makin' cotton gins, cars and skyscrapers goin' up. You name it. Unfortunately, this splendid age of manly things was tarnished by the Manfraction. One large sector of Manfractions was in the textile industry. With inventions like the "spinning jenny" and the "flyer and bobbin" it's not too much of a stretch to imagine some guy named Horatio frettin' over what colors look good together and the proper thread count for sheets. The world has not been the same since.

The 1970s

These were very manly and macho times for the most part, with hairy chests and leisure suits. Men exuded manliness based on the examples of Shaft, Dirty Harry and Barry White. However, we should not forget about some very egregious examples of Manfractions. Who can forget disco and those guys wearin' bellbottom pants. How about those dudes who coordinated outfits with their wives and girlfriends?

The 1980s

Sure, we had our positive role models like Ronald Reagan and Thomas Magnum but we also had those Heavy Metal Hair bands. The 80's Glam Rock scene was a hornet's nest of Manfractions. Those guys spent way too much time gettin' ready. They wore makeup, flowin' scarves and spandex. Who could forget the decade that brought us all of those pastels for our homes and apparel courtesy of Miami Vice. Hey, there was even a band in the 80s called LoverBoy – 'nuff said.

Information Age (Present Economic Era)

Overall, lots of benefits for the man. Cable TV, baseball statistics online, 24 hour sports channels. Record that fishin' show while you're at church. Track your team's draft picks durin' the offseason. In short, lots of ways for men to get the things that matter to them such as sports scores, swimsuit issues and Internet porn. However, for the man there's also a dark side. All this information can be confusin'. When flippin' through all those channels you can sometimes come across things that make you feel a little strange such as infomercials on male pattern baldness, or Oprah. One commercial tells you to smell good while another tells you to drive a big ol' truck – what's a man to do!?

Metrosexual Age (Present Cultural Era)

This is the age in which we're strugglin' today. Without a doubt, these days, men are spendin' way too much time and money attendin' to their personal appearance. Some men even watch shows like "What Not to Wear." Men have excessive products in their bathrooms. They are goin' to salons to get highlights put in their hair. They're gettin' manicures for Goodness sake. What has the world come to?

Although Manfractions have surfaced throughout history, it is the confluence of the information age with the metrosexual age that broke the proverbial camel's back for us. It's a vicious circle. Men are doin' unmanly things and because (thanks to the information age) they see others doin' similarly unmanly things they think it's OK. The explosion of unmanly acts creates the illusion that those acts are acceptable. Well, we are here to tell you that they are not! The purpose of this book is to acknowledge the amount of ground we've given up and to definitively say these acts are not OK. Guys, now is the time to take our manhood back!

The rest of this book outlines Manfractions based on a number of different categories. From your body, to your ride, the followin' pages tell you the activities that constitute Manfractions. Make this a careful and thoughtful read because when you're done there will be a scenario-based exam to test your knowledge. We encourage you to take this test to see how much you've learned but the true test will be how you live the rest of your life after you read this book!

1. YOUR BODY

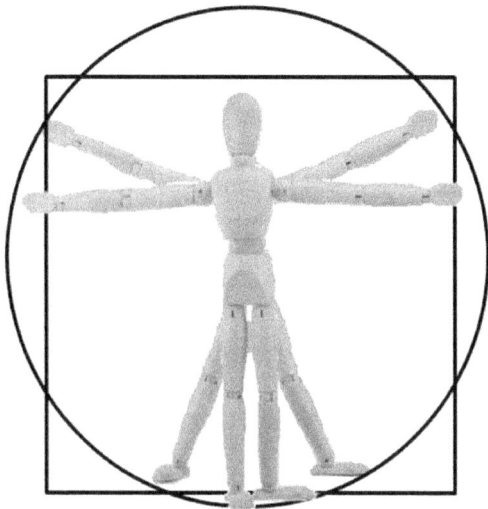

We all came into this world in our birthday suits. For men, that's usually good enough.   But these days, there's a tendency for men to not be satisfied with the package God gave 'em. Men have been known to modify their bodies for a number of reasons. From a Manfraction standpoint, some are good and some, well, not so much.

Why is this important? It is simply because how you look and how you carry yourself is the single most important reflection of your manliness to the outside world. Let's get started.

Tattoos

Usually a very manly thing...a good ol' skull tattoo, a biker tattoo...and there's pain involved! Be careful though, what kind of tatt you get can raise some questions. Check these out.

♂ **Lower back tattoos**. You've got to be kiddin'?! It's a target! Are you in receive mode? Do you want dudes lookin' down there? Even if you have sleeves of tattoos, avoid the general lower back area. Don't you know that lower back tattoos are also referred to as "Tramp Stamps" and "Reading Material." End of story.

♂ **Flower tattoos**. Do we really have to explain this?

♂ **Butterfly tattoos**. Hey Nancy boy...pull up your skirt.

♂ **Unicorn tattoos**. Wait a minute...what's that sound? It's your mommy callin' you.

♂ **Dolphin tattoos**. Don't laugh, they're out there. We don't care if you like Don Shula or Dan Marino – tattooin' a dolphin on your body is a Manfraction. If you're gettin' a shark tattoo, make damn sure your shark doesn't look like a dolphin!

♂ **Ankle tattoos**. Not very manly and you have to bend over to see it!

♂ **Painted-on tattoos**. What's wrong, can't ya take a little pain?

♂ _____

♂ _____

♂ _____

♂ _____

♂ _____

♂ _____

♂ _____

♂ _____

♂ _____

♂ _____

♂ _____

♂ _____

♂ _____
♂ _____
♂ _____

Hair

♂ **Comb-over**. There's a classic "Deep Thoughts by Jack Handey" quote: "If you ever drop your keys into a river of molten lava, let 'em go, because, man they're gone." This same logic applies to your hair. Just let it go, because, man, it's gone.

♂ **Toupee**. Even worse than the comb over. Wigs are for chicks, period.

♂ **Mousse**. Goop in your hair...out of a whipped cream can? Sorry...girls only.

♂ **Hairspray**. It's just not that important that every hair stay in place.

♂ **Blow dryers**. All that time and effort -- and for what? A little fluffy hair? If you need one of these things, your hair's too long anyway.

♂ **Usin' any hair growin' medicine.** When you're buyin' that box of hair growth medication you might as well pick up a box of tampons while you're at it.

♂ **Gettin' a perm**. First, you shouldn't be goin' to a salon. Second you shouldn't let someone put curlers in your hair.   Third, perms are not options at traditional barbershops.

♂ _____
♂ _____
♂ _____
♂ _____
♂ _____
♂ _____

♂ _____
♂ _____
♂ _____
♂ _____
♂ _____
♂ _____
♂ _____
♂ _____
♂ _____

Jewelry

♂ **Bracelets**. Never put anythin' on your wrist that does not perform a function or pay tribute. Watches are OK. So, too, are wrist tributes to Prisoners of War (POW) or those who are Missing in Action (MIA). Lance Armstrong's "Live Strong" wristbands are also acceptable. But don't go overboard. Use a maximum of one. Sweatbands also are OK because they perform a valid sportin' function.

♂ **Pinky ring(s)**. All frill...no function.

♂ **Cufflinks**. Rooster Cogburn never wore cufflinks.

♂ **Glasses**. Make sure you don't buy a pair that looks like ladies glasses. Never buy designer glasses. Bright colors, charms and a chain to carry them on your neck are all Manfractions.

♂ **Piercings**. Any and all piercings are Manfractions. Ear, lip, eyebrow, tongue...we don't care where it is or how much it hurt, they're all Manfractions.

♂ **Watches**. Be careful here. Watches say a lot about a man. Black Timex and multi-instrument pilot watches always work. Anythin' with diamonds or more than four roman numerals on the face are strictly verboten.

♂ _____

♂ _____

♂ _____

♂ _____

♂ _____

♂ _____

♂ _____

♂ _____

♂ _____

♂ _____

♂ _____

♂ _____

♂ _____

♂ _____

♂ _____

♂ _____

<u>Miscellaneous.</u>

♂ **Pattin' your mouth when yawnin'**. When you yawn, just yawn. If you don't want others to see your tonsils, bring your fist to your mouth. An open hand is wrong, an open hand that is pattin' is even worse. If you make noise when you yawn, you should make sure the pitch is low. Growl like a bear, don't sing like a bird.

♂ **Plastic surgery**. Unless there's some medical necessity, men do not go under the knife to improve their looks.[3]

♂ **Botulinum toxin injections**. Wrinkles are the scars of time. Embrace your life experience, don't run from it.

---

[3] Man boobs offer one counterexample. You're gonna get endless crap for 'em. If you ever wind up in prison, you'll be somebody's bitch. Self-preservation requires that you get those hooters cut off.

♂ **Collagen injections**. Stop worryin' about your thin lips and go get a huntin' license.

♂ **Makeup**. Men should not wear makeup. News guys and politicians are doin' this all the time and it's makin' us sick.[4]

♂ **Crossin' your legs at the knee**. If you have to cross your legs, your ankle should rest on the knee. This act is much worse if you rock your leg.

♂ **Lickin' your lips**. If someone points out that you have food on your mouth, don't lick. Wipe your mouth with your arm.

♂ **Fannin' your mouth or screamin' when your food's too hot**. A real man does not let on to others that the flesh inside his mouth is burnin' from food that is too hot or spicy. Instead, he should casually use his drink to neutralize the pain. Make sure you learn the appropriate lesson from each incident so you're better prepared for the next time.

♂ **Impotence in an era of pharmaceutical alternatives**. You might have been askin' yourself if takin' male enhancement drugs is a Manfraction. No way! Those little pills are all about gettin' your manhood back!

♂ **Usin' bandages for minor cuts and scrapes**. Don't hide your battle scars – be proud.

♂ **Wearin' a child's bandage**. See above. If you have to use a bandage, make sure it is a basic variety. Don't use the ones with cartoon characters on them.

♂ _____

♂ _____

---

[4] The only acceptable exception is paintin' yourself up for the big game. Body paint is man's modern-day equivalent of war paint. It is not makeup.

2. YOUR CLOTHES

What you wear, or don't wear, is a definite clue to your manliness. It's an outward sign to the world that you are a man and you don't care who knows. And when the clothes start to come off? Well, you know the rest. Here's a list of the clothing Manfractions.

- ♂ **One word...pink.**[5] Anythin' pink is a clear Manfraction. One exception...the pink breast cancer ribbon. It's for a fantastic cause...and hey, you're savin' breasts! What could be manlier?
- ♂ **Shoes with tassels**. Need we say more?
- ♂ **Suspenders**. Also known as braces. Whatever you call them, we call them Manfractions. Wear a belt, one with a big, honkin' buckle like the Pro Bull Riders wear (now these are some real men).
- ♂ **Garters**. Some guys wear these to keep their shirts in and their socks up. Let it hang out and let 'em sag!
- ♂ **Vests**. We're not talkin' about those worn with your 3-

---

[5] This Manfraction also applies to other areas as well. For example, pink cars, pink furniture, pink music players, pink drinks, pink cell phones...you get the picture.

piece suit. Vests worn alone or over a shirt are forbidden. Unless you're Trace Adkins, don't do it.

♂ **Leather pants**. Leather chaps for ridin' your Harley, okay. Leather pants for a night out on the town? Please.

♂ **Fancy leather sandals**. 'Nuff said.

♂ **Penny loafers**. Too preppy, not enough cojones.

♂ **Tightie whities**. You're not in 3rd grade anymore, wear boxers.

♂ **Puffy Clothes**. The only thing that should be puffy on you is that shiner you got defendin' your woman's honor.

♂ **Clam diggers**. It may be a Manfraction just knowin' what these damn things are.

♂ **Rubber clogs with holes**. No way! Call a compound Manfraction if you see a man wearin' these things with little shiny metal charms.

♂ **Scandinavian winter knit hats**. The ones with the earflap tassels. Hey man, you might as well grow your hair long and braid it.

♂ **Mittens**. What are you, five years old? Be a man!

♂ **Slippers**. Unless you're in the Playboy mansion, there is no rational man-reason to wear these things.

♂ **Scarf**. We're gonna barf if we catch you wearin' a scarf!

♂ **Ascot**. Wearin' silky fabric next to your skin is not very macho. Plus, the first part of the word has "ass" in it.

♂ **Earmuffs**. It is better to have frozen ears than commit this Manfraction. Nothin' says I'm a delicate wimp more than a pair of earmuffs.[6]

♂ **Berets**. Unless you're in the Army or a member of the special forces, don't wear these things. Prince sang about 'em for God's sake.

♂ **Half shirts or mesh shirts**. What, do you want the boys to check out your abs?

♂ **Tank tops**. Some guys call 'em 'muscle shirts' we call 'em wrong.

♂ **Super small swimsuits**. Unless you're an Olympic-caliber swimmer, you should never go near these things.

♂ **Designer Jeans**. Fancy stitchin' on the back pockets, rhinestones, etc., are not allowed.

♂ **Boots with zippers**. We'll bet if you watch all of John Wayne's movies you'll never see him with zippers on his boots.

♂ **Superbowl jacket with rhinestones.** A Super Bowl jacket is cool, right? You want to celebrate because your team won the big game. They are World Champions! Just make sure you don't have any sparkles on that jacket.

♂ **Thongs**. Both kinds...underwear and footwear.

♂ **Carryin' your jacket over the shoulder**. Are you practicin' your runway walk?

♂ **Tyin' your sweater around your neck**. This is just ridiculous. You don't tie your socks around your ankles, do you?

♂ **Anything tight or "formfittin'."**

♂ **Huge shoe collection**. Men should not have an Imelda

---

[6] Please keep the self-preservation clause in mind here. If you're stranded in a blizzard and earmuffs will keep your ears from fallin' off or save your life, put 'em on!

Marcos-sized collection. Please fellas, no more than two pairs of non-athletic shoes.

♂ **Turtlenecks**. They're like a permanent scarf.

♂ **Wearin' a shirt or jacket with the collar turned up**. Elvis had it goin' on, you don't…put your collar down.

♂ **Providin' unsolicited clothing advice**.   Other than enforcin' the rules, you are not to make apparel recommendations to your fellow man. You can (and should) tell him to stop wearin' spandex, but you should not tell him that a light blue shirt "would look better and bring out his eyes."

♂ **Sweaters with hearts, flowers and/or kissin' birds**. Let's face it fellas, we can't control the gifts we get but we can control what we choose to wear.

♂ **Corduroy**. Sorry Professor…Manfraction.

♂ **Fur (real or fake)**. Unless you live in the Arctic Circle and need it to survive frigid temperatures, men shall not wear any fur, period. Back in the day, men wearin' fur was acceptable and rather manly but today we have Gortex and other technologies to keep us warm.

♂ **Cartoon character clothes**. You know, wearin' clothes that have cartoon characters imprinted on them (large or small). This may be OK for the ladies and the little ones but it is not OK for men!

♂ **Blanket with sleeves**. You've probably seen these advertised on TV over the holidays – not very manly.

♂ _____

♂ _____

♂ _____

♂ _____

♂ _____

♂ _____

♂ _____

♂ _____

♂ _____

♂ _____

♂ _____

♂ _____

♂ _____

♂ _____

♂ _____

3. MAN-COMM

The way you communicate (either verbally or non-verbally) sends a message to others about your manhood. We like to call this man-comm. Men talk to men in a certain way. It's almost like a different language.[7] For you real men out there, we've included the definitions for some of these words with which you may not be familiar. Sayin', writin' or doin' these Manfractions will make your buddies think twice about invitin' you to poker night.

Forbidden Words

♂ **Bistro**. Translated, this word means "small restaurant or bar." Just use those terms, no need to get fancy.

♂ **Bunny**. Unless your talkin' 'bout one of Heff's bunnies, this word is not allowed.

♂ **Bye, bye**. Unless you're talkin' to your little kid, never say this one.

♂ **Canasta**. This is a card game your wife plays with her friends.

---

[7] Next to smoke signals, Morse code may be the most manly forms of man-comm. No frill, no grammar…just dots and dashes.

- **Chartreuse**. This is a color.[8]
- **Croissant**. If you have to say this French word out loud you better pronounce it "Cresint." Otherwise, you are what you eat – soft and flaky.
- **Dazzle**. You're just kiddin' us, right?
- **Ditto**. Especially on email when taggin' on to another man's backin' out of a party invite (Hey, you're givin' up free beer!).
- **Dollop**. "Just a dollop of whip cream in my pumpkin spice latte, please."
- **Duvet**. [doo·vay] (noun). *A type of bed quilt. A bed quilt made up of broad channels stuffed with down or synthetic material, usually used inside a removable washable cover in place of or together with sheets and blankets.*
- **Emoticons**. Those little happy/sad faces in emails…e.g., :-), :-(, ;-), :o, etc. Please note that ":o" is the most heinous of emoticons for a man to use.
- **Ewwww**. Oh, I'm sorry, did you see a mouse! Man-up sissy-boy.
- **Fabulous**. As in, "This outfit is fabulous."
- **Fluffy**. We can't image Rooster Cogburn or Harry Callahan sayin' this.
- **Fuzzy**. e.g. "warm fuzzy," "fuzzy slippers," etc.
- **Gee Wilickers**. Yeah, right!
- **Gee Whiz**. See "Gee Wilickers."
- **Goblet**. Sayin' goblet is just as bad as drinkin' out of

---

[8] The original "Crayola 8" are really the only acceptable colors for a man to reference. They are: black, blue, brown, green, orange, red, purple, and yellow. For example, Jeep had a color for their "Grand Cherokee" in the mid 90's called "light driftwood satin glow." You better just call it brown.

one.

○⚥ **Golly**. Are you pretendin' to be talkin' to the Beave?!

○⚥ **Gorgeous**. As in, "those curtains look gorgeous!"

○⚥ **Gosh**. See Golly.

○⚥ **Jammies**. e.g. "I'm tired, I think I'm going to put on my jammies."

○⚥ **Lovely**. "Those flowers would look lovely on my mantel."

○⚥ **Luv**. We don't care if it saves you a keystroke. Don't do it!

○⚥ **Mauve**. Another color.

○⚥ **Oops** or **Whoops**. Not only do you sound like a pansy…"Oopsie!"…but you're apologizin'. Not too manly.

○⚥ **Oops…sorry**. You'd be amazed at how many men say this.

○⚥ **Owwieee**. Do you want us to get your Mommy so she can kiss it for you?

○⚥ **Periwinkle**. Believe it or not, this is another color.

○⚥ **Precious**. Isn't that little kitty just precious?

○⚥ **Quiche**. [keesh] – noun. *a pie like dish consisting of an unsweetened pastry shell filled with a custard and usually containing cheese and other ingredients, as vegetables, seafood, or ham: spinach quiche.* Don't say it, don't eat it.

○⚥ **Silly**. As in, "Stop it, you silly!"

○⚥ **Soliloquy**. [so·lil·o·quy] noun. *Talking when alone. The act of speaking while alone, especially when used as a theatrical device that allows a character's thoughts and ideas to be conveyed to the audience.*

○⚥ **Sprinkles**. Don't say sprinkles, don't eat sprinkles, don't name your dog Sprinkles.

♂ **Spritz**. For example, "I'll have a martini with a spritz."

♂ **Super**. e.g. "that outfit looks super."

♂ **Ta, ta**. If you're leavin' a buddy's house, just give the head nod and say "See ya'." Now if you're talkin' no kidding Ta-Tas (i.e. Hooters, Jugs, Boobs) well then, okay.

♂ **Tasty**. "These meatballs are very tasty."

♂ **Tee-he** or **Tee-he-he**. Please.

♂ **Thanx**. You're not savin' that much time by usin' an "x" instead of a "ks." Are you tryin' to be cute?

♂ **Tinkle**.

♂ **Tizzy**. e.g. "I'm so upset that I've worked myself into a tizzy."

♂ **Touché**. [too·sháy] noun. *An acknowledgment of a telling remark or of scoring a hit.*

♂ **Twinkle**.

♂ **Uh oh**. e.g. "Un oh, I forgot to pack my slippers."

♂ **Vis-à-vis**. [vee-zuh-vee; Fr. vee-za-vee] adverb, adjective, preposition, noun, plural in relation to; compared with: income vis-à-vis expenditures. Huh? We still don't get it?!

♂ **Sayin' "I'll be there with bells on"**. Are you kiddin' me, are you goin' to show up in your tights too?

♂ **Yummy**. e.g. "Those crepes are really yummy!"

♂ **Euro-spellings**. Shoppe, Sporte, Defence. English is tough enough as is. Don't confuse things by tryin' to be cute or worldly.

♂ **Certain Pronunciations.** For example: (1) Pronouncin' *Schedule* as *Shed-yule;* (2) Pronouncin' *Foyer* as *Foy-yeah;* (3) Pronouncin' *Croissant* as *Cwa-saunt, or worse, craw-saw.*

♂ _____
♂ _____
♂ _____
♂ _____
♂ _____
♂ _____
♂ _____
♂ _____
♂ _____
♂ _____
♂ _____
♂ _____
♂ _____
♂ _____
♂ _____

Forbidden Statements and Gestures

♂ **Askin' another dude what his sign is**. What...is he cute?

♂ **Sayin' you're "on holiday"**. Hey Pal, in America we go on vacation.

♂ **Wavin'**. Wavin' with the hand above the shoulder is particularly bad. Wavin' with the hand above the shoulder while standin' or bouncin' on your tippy toes is worse still. Men nod, point or shake hands, they don't wave.

♂ **Winkin' at another dude**. Just a little joke between buddies? Next thing you know you'll be swappin' recipes or givin' each other backrubs. Don't even go there.

♂ **Wishin' "happy valentine's day" to another man**. Valentine's Day is a holiday men should not acknowledge in public.

♂ **Signalin' another man to "come here" with your finger**. There is absolutely no excuse for this kind of freakish behavior.

♂ **Pinky wave**. One of us saw this once when a dude had his hands full while talkin' on the cell phone. Instead of acknowledgin' another individual with the typical head nod upward, this "guy" proceeded to wave with his pinky. God help us!

♂ **Holdin' a phone up to another dude's ear**. If your pal has his hands full and gets a call he should put his things down and take the call himself. Under no circumstances should you hold the phone to his ear for him. That's a clear violation of man-spacin' and – to be honest – is just bizarre!

♂ _____

♂ _____

♂ _____

♂ _____

♂ _____

♂ _____

♂ _____

♂ _____

♂ _____

♂ _____

♂ _____

♂ _____

♂ _____

♂ _____

♂ _____

4. YOUR NAME

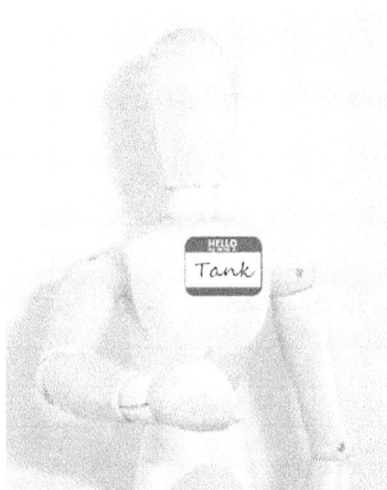

Let's face it. We didn't get to choose our names but we can change them.[9] If you have any of the followin' names (or if you thinkin' about namin' your son one of these) you're committin' a Manfraction.

♂ **Bruce**. Sorry, Bruce, just too much "ssss" at the end.[10]

♂ **Neil**. Somethin' real men should never do

♂ **Robin, Tracey, Kim, Adrian, etc**. There are a lot of good dudes out there with these names but if a chick has the same name as you then we have a problem, don't we?

---

[9] Note: The Appendix describes the very manly and practical ritual of the call sign namin' ceremony.

[10] Bruce Smith (former NFL defensive end) also as a lot of "ssss" in his name but if you value your health we don't recommend you call him out.

♂ **Men who hyphenate their last names**. Tradition clearly has the woman takin' the man's last name. Attachin' your new wife's maiden name to yours is clearly out of bounds. Although it may make mamma happy, you cannot do it – after all, it is part of the permanent record!

♂ **Men who take their wife's maiden names upon marriage**. Don't laugh...it's happened.

♂ _____

♂ _____

♂ _____

♂ _____

♂ _____

♂ _____

♂ _____

♂ _____

♂ _____

♂ _____

♂ _____

♂ _____

♂ _____

♂ _____

♂ _____

5. YOUR PET

Your choice of a pet tells us a lot about how much of a man you are. Pets should fulfill a purpose. Huntin' dogs come to mind here. If you want to be a man you need to stay away from the followin' pets -- don't own one, don't look at them, never pet them.

- ♂ **Poodles**. If it's curly and white you have no right.
- ♂ **Any toy breed**. Dogs are not toys and should be bigger than your foot.
- ♂ **Designer dogs**. Like the ones that could fit in a purse. Nice pooch, Paris!
- ♂ **Cats**. Especially single guys with cats. C'mon! We know of a single dude who has his cat on his answerin' machine…"Fluffy and I aren't home right now…" Are you kiddin'?
- ♂ **Pet clothes**. For example, dressin' your dog up in a Halloween costume or puttin' a sweater on it before you take it out for a walk.
- ♂ **Snakes**. It's OK if you feed 'em rodents, but don't pet 'em in public.
- ♂ **Hamsters or other rodents**. These are kid's pets. Plus we've all heard about those freaky rumors.
- ♂ **Rabbit**. Too fluffy and they can't do tricks.
- ♂ **Ferrets**. You can't take these things huntin'.
- ♂ **Pony**. Get a horse but whatever you do, don't obsess over it and don't wear knickers and ridin' pants.
- ♂ **Sheep or Goats**. What will the neighbors think?
- ♂ _____
- ♂ _____
- ♂ _____

♂ _____

♂ _____

♂ _____

♂ _____

♂ _____

♂ _____

♂ _____

♂ _____

♂ _____

♂ _____

♂ _____

♂ _____

6. AT HOME

You're the King of your castle, not the Queen. Even though you may be alone, you must always live the rules! Never do or have the followin':

♂ **Knitted Toilet Paper Holder**. Under no circumstances should such a device be allowed to hang in any bathroom occupied by a man. If you see one of these you should immediately exit the premises.

♂ **Toilet accessories**. Hey, toilets are for two things (three if you've had too much to drink). Don't make them out to be more than they are.

♂ **Doll collections**. Havin' dolls or displayin' dolls in your home is a Manfraction. How can you bring the fellas over to watch the game when there is a porcelain freak show on display? We don't care if it makes momma happy, sack-up cowboy.

♂ **Action figures**. Are you still livin' in your parent's basement?

♂ **Stuffed animals**. Newsflash. You're not 5 anymore and neither is your wife/girlfriend.

♂ **Girly rooms**. Your livin' room better not have multiple shades of pink and anythin' frilly. If so, you may want to set up permanent residence in the garage.

♂ **Fleur-de-le**. They have a phallic, flowery shape. Plus, they're French. Strictly off limits!

♂ **Bakin'**. Man has to eat but he cannot get carried away in the kitchen. This includes bakin' cakes, cookies, pastries and soufflés. If you really need this stuff, get it at the bakery section of your grocery store. If you're cookin', it better be outside on the grill. Under no circumstances should you wear an apron.

♂ **Wearin' an apron**. See "Bakin'."

♂ _____

♂ _____

♂ _____

♂ _____

♂ _____

♂ _____

♂ _____

♂ _____

♂ _____

♂ _____

♂ _____

♂ _____

♂ _____

♂ _____

♂ _____

7. YOUR FREE TIME

Your free time is too valuable to be caught doin' the followin':

♂ **Sewin'**. Makin' clothes, drapes, or pillows.[11]

♂ **Dancin'**.[12]   Whether it's ballroom, country, etc. The only time ballroom should enter your mind is when you correctly decide to buy boxers over briefs.

♂ **Shoppin'**. This is not somethin' you should enjoy. Know what you're gonna to buy, buy it, and get out. No browsin'.

♂ **Enterin' a dance contest**. This includes participatin' in the "Dancing with the Stars" TV show. We don't care if you're the NFL's all-time leadin' rusher or a boxin' champion. You come on this show (or watch this show) and you're committin' a Manfraction.

♂ **Attendin' a baby shower**. There are some rituals that should never be witnessed by man.

♂ **Playin' bunco or mahjong**. These games are for chicks only.

♂ **Goin' to the movies with your buddy**.[13] Sittin' right next to him is worse. Again, you must maintain the proper man-spacin'.

---

[11] The only possible exception for sewing is if you're reupholsterin' your car seats or a leather chair for your man cave.

[12] This raises an interesting question. When is it appropriate for men to dance? Here are some possible acceptable scenarios. (1) You're dancing for money on the street – i.e. dancing for survival. (2) You're dancing with a gun to your head (also dancing for survival). (3) You're dancing at your own wedding or one of your children's weddings.

[13] When it comes to Manfractions, there's safety in numbers. When you're out with the boys, try to stay in packs of at least three.

○⚦ **Card games like bridge, hearts or canasta**. The only acceptable card games are poker and blackjack. Just sayin' canasta is a Manfraction.

○⚦ **Tandem skydivin' with another dude**. Let's face it fellas...this just doesn't look right. Imagine how long it would take to strap yourself to the other guy. It brings new meanin' to the mile high club.

○⚦ **Tandem horseback ridin' with another dude**. Wade Boggs did this in 1996 after a New York Yankees World Series Win. He mounted a police horse and rode right behind one of New York City's finest.

○⚦ **Tandem bikin' with another dude**. This is worse than skydivin' because of the tight, colorful biker clothes, less danger, and the fact that the face of the "guy" on back is just inches from the butt sweat of the dude up front.

○⚦ **Scrapbookin'**. No man should be proficient in usin' pinking shears or a hot glue gun.

○⚦ **Buyin', sellin' or collectin' fancy baskets**. First off, baskets, in general, are not very manly (think Little Red Ridin' Hood). Secondly, these things are way too expensive. You could buy 5-6 twelve packs of beer for the cost of one basket – wake up man!

○⚦ **Certain tandem projects**. Warning. Some manly activities quickly lose that macho factor if you do them in certain ways. For example, when you're hangin' pictures or cabinets you must not stand right behind another man.

○⚦ **Rollerbladin'**. Hey, we don't care how you align the wheels, it's still roller skatin'.

○⚦ **Collectin' toys, comic books, action figures, etc**. These are not "investments" or "commodities," these are toys.

♂ **Wine tastin'**. Red and white should be the extent of your knowledge on wine. If you're talkin' 'bout nutty overtones, you've gone too far!

♂ **Gourmet cookin'**. Men eat to survive and because they're hungry. We don't care 'bout how it looks on the plate.

♂ **Makin' floral arrangements**. Real flowers or silk flowers...leave this to the ladies.

♂ **Gardenin'**. You should plant stuff once and maintain as required to keep it alive or within neighborhood covenant regulations. If you revisit the plant more than once per week, your gardenin'.

♂ _____

♂ _____

♂ _____

♂ _____

♂ _____

♂ _____

♂ _____

♂ _____

♂ _____

♂ _____

♂ _____

♂ _____

♂ _____

♂ _____

♂ _____

8. YOUR PROFESSION

DANGER
HARD HAT
AREA

Your choice of a profession tells us a lot about you. Certain jobs require a significant investment in time and resources. You have to get trainin' or go to school. In many respects, your profession becomes your identity and your legacy. Choose wisely. The followin' professions are Manfractions:

♂ **Male nurse**.[14] Sorry, society is not quite ready for this one yet. If you're sick, the last thing you want is a dude comin' in to check your temperature.

♂ **Male figure skater**. The outfits alone make this very, very wrong. It gets worse when you add the sissy struts and the fact that you have to collect the flowers and stuffed animals that fans throw at you.

---

[14] The fact that you need to put "male" in front of any job title should be a clue that you're gonna get endless crap. Did you see the movie "Meet the Parents"? Interestingly, any job with "man" at the end is a good and manly. For example, fireman, policeman, journeyman, foreman, etc.

♂ **Male cheerleader**. Sorry Mr. President, men should not prance along the sidelines rootin' on other men. Bein' able to hoist and hang out with the female cheerleaders is no excuse. Newsflash...those cheerleaders want the quarterback, not you.

♂ **Male flight attendant**. Bub-bye.

♂ **Male gymnast**. Same man-logic applies.

♂ **Male dancer**. Tights, leotards, pointy shoes and way too much flouncing!

♂ **Sellin' makeup or workin' as a makeup artist**. Men and makeup are not meant to go together.

♂ **Interior designer**. Any job where you have to be an expert in textures, fabrics and color combinations should be a clue to keep your distance.

♂ **Landscape designer**. This is a tough one. On one hand there's dirt, holes, trucks and concrete involved but on the other there's flowers. If you're one of these we recommend you call yourself a "Landscaper" or a "Landscape Architect."

♂ **Lawyer**. Sorry, we couldn't resist takin' a shot at lawyers.

♂ **Midwife**. Dude...please!

♂ **Nanny**. WTF?

♂ **Hairstylist**. Rollers, hairspray and gossip. "...then Mary told Betty to keep away from her man ..."

♂ **Popsicle salesman**. Not very manly.

♂ **Hotdog on a stick salesman**. See "Popsicle salesman."

♂ **Chocolate Covered Banana Salesman**. See Hotdog on a stick salesman.

♂ **Instructor or trainer for any of the above professions**. This is worse because of the extra time and dedication it takes.

♂ _____
♂ _____
♂ _____
♂ _____
♂ _____
♂ _____
♂ _____
♂ _____
♂ _____
♂ _____
♂ _____
♂ _____
♂ _____
♂ _____
♂ _____

Places to Not Work[15]

♂ **Sellin' those mini European cars**. How, in good conscience, can you sell these tiny machines to other men?

♂ **Clothing store at the mall**. We can't think of any justification or clause that would allow this.

♂ **Bayer aspirin factory**. Sorry, there's a "bare ass" in the name.

♂ **Flower shop**.

♂ _____
♂ _____

---

[15] We should mention admirable places for men to work. These include: (1) ManTech (you know these guys are havin' off-sites at the sports bar; (2) Booz Allen Hamilton (you can tell people you're workin' for Booz!); (3) Any brewery, Duh!; (4) Jackhammer operator, (5) Hockey player, etc.

♂ _____
♂ _____
♂ _____
♂ _____
♂ _____
♂ _____
♂ _____
♂ _____
♂ _____
♂ _____
♂ _____
♂ _____
♂ _____

Things Not to Do at Work

♂ **Excessively apologizin' to your wife or girlfriend on the phone**. The cubical walls are pretty thin pal. Take it outside.

♂ **Askin' another dude to go to lunch with you.** Remember to do in packs of three or more.

♂ **Usin' a big rubber ball as an office chair**. No joke...we've seen this.

♂ **Askin' another man to walk over to the gourmet coffee shop**. Are you goin' to hold hands and skip along the way?

♂ _____
♂ _____
♂ _____
♂ _____
♂ _____
♂ _____
♂ _____

9. YOUR RIDE

We all know that a car makes the man. Your ride says more about you than pretty much anythin' else you own. Chicks come out of the woodwork when you pull up to the casino in a high-end European sports car; they disappear just as fast when you drive up in a Hybrid. Take a look at these vehicular-Manfractions.

♂ **Those mini-English cars**. Hey dude, wakeup! You're drivin' your wife's car.

♂ **Motorized scooters**. Some guys buy those big honkin' 600 CC scooters. Still a Manfraction.

♂ **Ridin' backseat on a motorcycle**. We all know who that seat's for...

♂ **Three dudes in the front seat of the truck**. That middle spot is reserved for your woman or your dog, period.

♂ **Hybrids**. Too small and wimpy. The only time a man

should plug in his car is to activate the block heater to keep the oil from freezin'.

○ **Minivans**. Make a pact with your buddies to never buy a minivan. Get an SUV instead. If you must get a van, get an old school van with shag carpet, mood lighting and a waterbed in the back.

○ **Those revamped mini-German cars**. Even without the flower accessories, it raises the question, doesn't it?

○ **Hangin' things from your rearview mirror**. Crystals, dream catchers, crystals, etc. Oooh, we wouldn't want to have a bad dream!

○ **Vanity plates**. EASYRDR, SHOEFRK, MANEATR. If your wife has these on her car you are never allowed to drive it or even ride in it. If you have these on your car, then we have another problem.

○ **Girly spare tire covers**. Smiley faces, cartoon characters, flowers, etc. Skulls and the American flag are OK.

○ **Flowery seat covers**. Recommend you patch those holes with duct tape instead.

○ **Stallin' your ride**. What, are you a chick – can't drive a stick?

○ **Addin' a gel seat cover to your mountain bike**. This is like wearin' a raincoat in the shower – sort of defeats the purpose...doesn't it?

○ **Tandem bicycle**. You're just invitin' company with one of these things. That extra spot better not be filled by a dude. If it's a chick, it looks like you're too weak to ride a bike by yourself.

○ **Two dudes in a convertible with the top down**. This works for Thelma & Louise. Not so much for Neil & Bob.

♂ **Stallin' your motorcycle**. If this happens, you should kick the bike over and just walk away.

♂ **Addin' a "bra" to your truck**. Preventin' minor chips and scratches is not that important. You might as well add some panties while you're at it.

♂ **Stuffed animals on the dashboard or behind the backseat**. That's just freaky.

♂ **Stuffed animal on the back of your motorcycle**. Nothin' kills that manly image you're goin' for like a little bear strapped to your motorcycle.

♂ **Antenna balls**. If you put a ball on your car's antenna, you may want to get a pair for yourself.

♂ **Skateboard**. OK if you are under 18 years old or if you are a professional.

♂ **Those two-wheeled, self-balancin' vehicles**. In addition to lookin' really weird, you can't take these things huntin'.

♂ **Lettin' your wife drive your Truck/SUV**. How can you be king of your castle when you can't be king of your vehicle?

♂ _____

♂ _____

♂ _____

♂ _____

♂ _____

♂ _____

♂ _____

♂ _____

♂ _____

♂ _____

♂ _____

♂ _____

♂ _____

♂ _____

♂ _____

10. AWAY FROM HOME

Bein' outside or on the road is a real test of your manhood. You're away from your comfort zone. You're surrounded by strangers. You may even be alone. It's OK to let your guard down, right? Wrong! Don't commit these Manfractions.

- ☿ **Askin' for directions**. You might as well ask for your Mommy. Here's a hint...get a map or GPS.
- ☿ **Usin' an umbrella**. Are you afraid the rain might mess up your hair or your clothes? This Manfraction increases in severity if you share that umbrella with another dude.
- ☿ **Bringin' shampoo on your campin' trip**. You're in the wilderness for Heaven's sake. You can go without washin' your hair for a few days. The same logic applies to other things such as pajamas or slippers.
- ☿ **Enterin' a drive-in carwash with your buddy**. Somethin' is just not right about this. What's the real difference between this and goin' on the "Tunnel of Love" ride at the State Fair with your best pal?
- ☿ **Sniffin' somethin' before you buy it**. Whether it's deodorant, laundry detergent or those scented candles your wife put on your shoppin' list. Don't worry about what it smells like, just buy it. Please, no sniffin' in public.
- ☿ **Runnin' with your arms pressed to your sides**. If you're crossin' the street or tryin' to catch a bus or plane you need to run like a man! Move those arms – it'll help you go faster and you won't look like a female gymnast.

♂ **Runnin' with limp or floppy wrists**. This is simply wrong and is a waste of valuable energy.

♂ **Runnin' or Joggin' like a girl**. Not a good idea.[16]

♂ **Gettin' your face painted**. If you're puttin' on your war paint for the big game, then OK. But if you just paid $3.50 to get that rainbow butterfly on your cheek, might as well go buy a matchin' bra.

♂ _____

♂ _____

♂ _____

♂ _____

♂ _____

♂ _____

♂ _____

♂ _____

♂ _____

♂ _____

♂ _____

♂ _____

♂ _____

♂ _____

♂ _____

[16] Similarly bad ideas include: screamin', whinin', laughin' or cryin' like a girl.

11. ON VACATION

Just because you're relaxin' doesn't mean you can suspend your duties as a man. Don't let us catch you doin' the followin' while on vacation.

☿ **Vegas shows**. Celine Deon, Elton John: The red piano, Barry Manilow: Music and Passion, Zumanity. Strip clubs yes, sissy shows, no way!

☿ **Spas**. No massages (unless you're just goin' for the happy ending!), no aromatherapy, no essential oils.[17]

☿ **Botanical or Butterfly gardens**.

☿ **Textile or clothing museum**. What's the point?

☿ **Plannin' your road trip based on outlet mall locations**. This is somethin' your wife may want to do but it better not be your idea!

☿ **Requestin' the middle seat in a bus or on a plane or train**. Under no circumstances should you seek to sit in the middle seat. Only do so out of necessity. You're only askin' for a couple of very uncomfortable hours should Neil or Bob sit next to you.

☿ **See "Haulin' Stuff" section for other examples**. e.g. bags on wheels, motorcycle trailers, etc.

_____

[17] One of the most heinous examples recently witnessed is a man gettin' a massage in the mall – in plain sight – from another dude. This is what we call a *compound Manfraction* – or a conglomeration of individual Manfractions where the whole is more egregious than the sum of the parts. In this case, let's call 'em out one at a time: (1) the guy was shopping at the mall; (2) this activity was so stressing that he had to stop and get relief; (3) he let another man touch him and rub him. Just readin' this should make you sick. This poor sap was basically sayin' "I want everyone in this mall to see what a pansy I really am."

12. AT THE GYM

Goin' to the gym, pumpin' iron, gettin' sweaty, stinkin' like a horse. It doesn't get any manlier than that...unless you commit a few of these winners.

Workout Gear

♂ **Spandex**. Glad to see you wearin' your wife's pants. Even if worn under a pair of shorts, even if you call 'em "compression shorts"...Manfraction.

♂ **Those little, flimsy runnin' shorts**. You are not Kip Keino.[18]

♂ **Black socks**. Nothin' says "I've never done this before" than wearin' black socks at the gym. The same goes for dress shoes, jeans, or button-down shirts.

♂ **Liftin' gloves**. You have a little bell on your bike, don't

---

[18] Who could forget Kip Keino's manly defeat of Jim Ryun in the 1500 meters at the 1968 Olympic Games after bein' disqualified from the 1000 meters for leavin' the track because of a gallbladder infection...rub some dirt on it Kip!

you?

⚥ **Headbands**. We have some news for you. The 70s are over. If you need to wipe the sweat from your brow, use your sleeve or a towel. Wipe, don't dab.

⚥ **Wearin' a backpack while exercisin'**. The only exception is if you're in the Army or the Corps.

⚥ **See "Your Clothes" section for other examples**. Tank tops, half shirts, mesh shirts, pink stuff, etc.

⚥ _____

⚥ _____

⚥ _____

⚥ _____

⚥ _____

⚥ _____

⚥ _____

⚥ _____

⚥ _____

⚥ _____

⚥ _____

⚥ _____

⚥ _____

⚥ _____

⚥ _____

In the Locker Room

⚥ **Bare assin' the bench**. Dude! What are you thinkin'? Other people are gonna use that bench!

⚥ **Bendin', stretchin', or otherwise exercisin' in the buff**. We don't wanna see that. We don't even wanna think about that!

⚥ **Walkin' around in the buff.** Put your towel on and get dressed as fast as you can. We don't need to see you like that!

♂ **Talkin' on your cell phone while in the buff**. What the hell!?

♂ **Lookin'**. Your head and eyes must stay straight ahead. Turn off your peripheral vision.

♂ **Improper spacin'**. In the shower or at the lockers, maintain the proper distance.

♂ **Sharin' a towel**. Dry off with your sweaty shirt if you have to.

♂ **Naked shavin', tooth brushin', etc**. Absolutely brutal! Wear a towel, please!

♂ **Too much talkin'**. There's a bunch of naked dudes all around you. Get dressed and take it outside.

♂ **Hangin' your towel on a hanger**. There is really no need to get so persnickety. You've used your towel, just wad it up and put it in your bag. If you want it to dry, drape it over your bag.

♂ **Puttin' baby powder on your junk**. Hey, you might as well put on a diaper and drink from a baby bottle. Man-up!

♂ **Askin' another dude to borrow his underarm deodorant**. Don't laugh…we've seen this actually take place and it was very disturbin'.

♂ **Runnin' into another man while walkin' to the shower**. You have to be very, very careful as you traverse the locker room. Again, wear your towel.

♂ _____

♂ _____

♂ _____

♂ _____

♂ _____

♂ _____

♂ _____
♂ _____
♂ _____
♂ _____
♂ _____
♂ _____
♂ _____
♂ _____
♂ _____

Workin' Out

♂ **Yoga**. We don't care if it kicks your ass. It just ain't right.

♂ **Pilates**. See Yoga

♂ **Jazzercise**. See Pilates

♂ **Ballet hands**. You've seen 'em. The chick instructor is tellin' you to breathe in with that little flick of the wrist. Don't do it!

♂ **Large colorful rubber balls (for workin' abs)**. Unless it's a sports ball or a medicine ball, stay away!

♂ **Power rods or big rubber bands**. Just go throw some weights around.

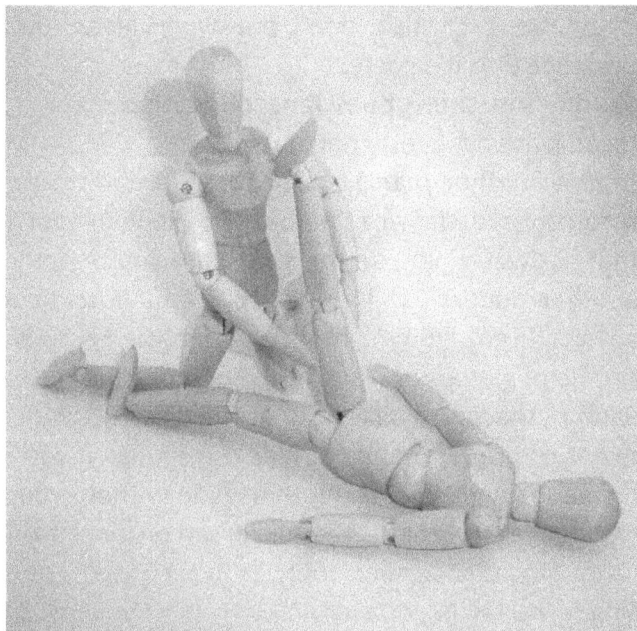

Men Helpin' Other Men Stretch.

♂ **Man-assisted stretchin'**. We don't care if you're a professional athlete. Figure out a way to stretch yourself or get a cheerleader to help you – not another man.

♂ **Bizarre stretches**. Men were not designed to perform the scorpion stretch. It's just not natural.

♂ **Things not to say when you're spottin' a lift**.
  o "Push it, yes...nice finish!"
  o "Give it to me man!"
  o "Faster, faster, ..."
  o "Thrust now..."

♂ **Excessive machine wipin'**. By all means, wipe your

sweat off the machine when you're done but don't get crazy about it. Also, don't pre-wipe unless you have evidence that it's nasty.

♂ **Sharin' the same pool lane durin' lap swim**. Hey, those lanes are pretty narrow.

♂ **Joinin' another man in hot tub**. We don't care how sore your muscles are. Before you dip your tootsies in that hot water, you better make sure you're not joinin' another dude. But hey, you don't have to take our advice. If not, you might as well dim the lights, pour a couple of glasses of wine and offer him a backrub.

♂ **Sauna spacin'**. Like other situations, you must maintain proper man-spacin' in the sauna. If you enter the sauna and there is another dude in there you have to select a spot that is the maximum distance from the other guy. Same rules apply as in the men's room, no singin', no talkin', no starin'.

♂ _____

♂ _____

♂ _____

♂ _____

♂ _____

♂ _____

♂ _____

♂ _____

♂ _____

♂ _____

♂ _____

♂ _____

♂ _____

♂ _____

♂ _____

Showerin'

♂ **Improper shower spacin'**. Under no circumstances will you stand next to another man while takin' a shower.

♂ **Nozzle too high**. Be aware of overspray. Water should not ricochet off you on to another man (or the other way around). You might as well just take a bath together.

♂ **Bendin' over**. 'Nuff said.

♂ **Excessive products**. What applies "in the Bathroom" at home is amplified in the shower "at the Gym." Don't be takin' a lot of products in there with you. One sport bottle of shampoo is plenty.

♂ **Singin'**. Hello, you're in public. Do you want people to think you're actually enjoyin' latherin' up with a bunch of naked dudes?

♂ _____

♂ _____

♂ _____

♂ _____

♂ _____

♂ _____

♂ _____

♂ _____

♂ _____

♂ _____

♂ _____

♂ _____

♂ _____

♂ _____

♂ _____

13. EATIN' AND DRINKIN'

Men know how to eat. It's one of the things we do best. Next to sex, it's what we think about most often. Why do you think they invented the all-you-can-eat buffet? If you spend your time eatin' sprouts or sippin' "cocktails", we're gonna start askin' some questions and callin' out Manfractions. Here are the forbidden food and drink behaviors.

Food
- ♂ **Crepes**. Why bother? You'd have to eat a million of 'em to fill up.
- ♂ **Cucumber sandwiches**. Does your husband know you're out?
- ♂ **Salad without a steak to back it up**. Salad is rabbit food. Eat like a man.
- ♂ **Bananas**. Be very careful how you eat these. No longing stares, no caressin' and no twistin'. Our advice…after peelin' just break off the pieces you want to eat.
- ♂ **Breadstick**. Same man-logic applies.
- ♂ **Ice cream cone**. Ditto.
- ♂ **Any meat on a stick**. Kabobs, Corndog…you get the picture. Take the meat off the stick and eat it with yer hands.
- ♂ **Yogurt**. Big guys look wimpy eatin' out of that little cup.
- ♂ **Soft-boiled egg**. Same man-logic as the cup of yogurt but even more so since soft-boiled eggs require a tiny spoon.
- ♂ **Quiche**. [keesh] – noun. *A pie like dish consisting of an*

unsweetened pastry shell filled with custard and usually containing cheese and other ingredients such as vegetables, seafood, or ham: e.g. spinach quiche.

⚣ **Signin' up for a weight loss program**. We don't care if the ex-football players are doin' it. These programs are for chicks only.

⚣ **Chicken nuggets**. Get chicken strips instead. You're over the age of 12 now.

⚣ **Any kids meal**. You're jokin', right?

⚣ **Wrap**. Be a man – eat a sandwich.

⚣ **Sprouts**. Not only should you not eat these things you shouldn't say the word either (way too much "sss").

⚣ **Rice cakes**. You might as well eat the Styrofoam packaging from those porcelain dolls you ordered.

⚣ **Muffalettas**. This may be the best tastin' sandwich ever, but you can never know because of the name alone. Under no circumstances should a man be caught sayin' (or eatin') this.

⚣ **"Holding" things**. Just order that burger. Don't hold the mayo, don't ask for sauce on the side.

⚣ **"Substituting" things**. You better not order a cup of fruit or a salad in place of those fries! Life's too short to worry that much. Fries are one of the five food groups, are they not?

⚣ **Bubble gum**. You can chew gum but don't smack it and don't blow bubbles.

⚣ **Fruit flavored cream cheese**. Do you really want to spread that stuff on your bagel? We don't think so.

⚣ **Countin' calories**. The addition of the nutrition label is a just another way for *The Man* to keep us down. Don't waste your time worryin' about this stuff. Just enjoy that bag of corn chips. Life's too short to be doin' math problems every time we get hungry.

♂ **Sprinkles**. Again, don't say sprinkles, don't eat sprinkles, don't name your dog Sprinkles.

♂ _____

♂ _____

♂ _____

♂ _____

♂ _____

♂ _____

♂ _____

♂ _____

♂ _____

♂ _____

♂ _____

♂ _____

♂ _____

♂ _____

♂ _____

Drink

♂ **Straws**. Unless you've got a "to-go cup", stay away from the straws. Dude, you're puttin' your lips on a long tube!

♂ **Sharin' a big drink with two or more straws**. This is particularly heinous if the person you're sharin' it with is another fella.[19]

♂ **Anything with "-ini" in it**. Martini, Appletini...c'mon, really!

─────────────────────

[19] In general, performin' any function with another dude in close proximity is a Manfraction and you see many examples in this book. Interestingly, the same cannot be said for activities that involve two women. That's just good scenery.

⚥ **Any specialty drink**. You know...cocktails. Especially those with props such as mini-umbrellas. Drinks like the Cucumber Cocktail, Electric Watermelon, Bahama Momma, African Lady, Blue Dolphin are clearly off limits. You get the picture. Acceptable man-drinks are scotch, whiskey and bourbon.

⚥ **Whip cream on your drink**. Too sissy.

⚥ **Fruit in your beer**. It's beer; it's not a fashion statement. Beer is perfectly fine the way it is. There's no real need to dress it up.

⚥ **Tall, fruity drinks**. With or without umbrellas...forget it. Men and anything "fruity" don't mix.

⚥ **Fresca**. Diet Fresca is worse.

⚥ **Complainin' about your drink bein' too strong**. What? Are you afraid you might get a little "tipsy"? Man-up, sissy boy and order another one.

⚥ **Complainin' about the brand of beer in your buddy's fridge**. Dude...it's beer and it's free. Get your head in the game!

⚥ **Drinkin' a diet shake**. Unless you're washin' it down with a Double Cheeseburger, that diet shake is not intended for men.

⚥ **Flavored coffee**. No man should order, let alone drink, a Caramel Frappuccino or a Pumpkin Spice Latte.[20]

⚥ **Mini cans of anything**. e.g. 6-ounce can of soda. What, are you afraid you're tummy will feel full if you drank a full-sized can?

---

[20] Hideous examples: Man drinks pink-colored gourmet coffee in a clear cup with whipped cream through a straw. This is also another example of a *compound Manfraction*. Breakin' it down we have: (1) drinkin' out of a straw; (2) holdin' and ingesting somethin' pink; (3) havin' whipped cream on a drink; (4) everyone can see you doin' this.

♂ **Mini coffee cups**. 12 ounces minimum.

♂ **Bottled water**. Hey pal, why pay for somethin' you can get for free? For a buck a bottle you could be drinkin' a beer.

♂ **Oversized coffee cups**. If it looks like a soup bowl with a handle, you must keep your distance.[21]

♂ _____

♂ _____

♂ _____

♂ _____

♂ _____

♂ _____

♂ _____

♂ _____

♂ _____

♂ _____

♂ _____

♂ _____

♂ _____

♂ _____

♂ _____

---

[21] As you can see, your coffee cup must meet specific man-standards. You also need to be very careful with coffee cup designs or pictures. No butterflies, flowers, etc. NASCAR images and pictures of animals you would hunt are OK. You get the picture.

14. HAULIN' STUFF

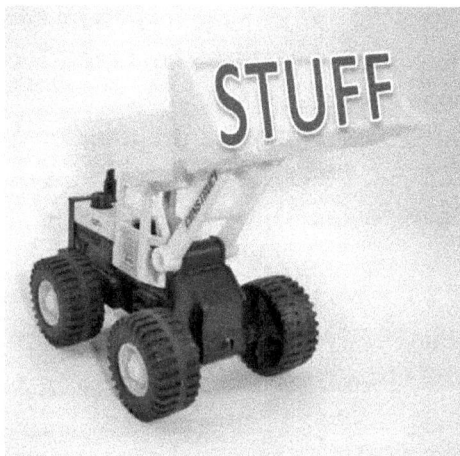

You're a man right? Men need to haul stuff. Let's make sure you're haulin' stuff the right way. Avoid these Manfractions.

♂ **Man-bag**. You call it a man-bag, we call it a purse. Purses are for women.

♂ **Fanny-pack**. You might call them wussy-packs or "I'm a sissy-pack." The name alone is a Manfraction.

♂ **Motorcycle trailers**. There's a shirt out there that says it all…"Nice trailer…you freakin' wussy!"

♂ **Soft-sided lunchbox**. Whatever happened to the old metal lunch box – you know, the ones with latches that were rusty inside and out and had curved lids?[22] Today we're seein' soft-sided, padded, lunch boxes with a shoulder strap. From a distance, it looks like a

---

[22] Another acceptable option is those hard plastic coolers that could survive a fall from a 10-story building. The dirtier the better!

purse. Carry your lunch in a leftover grocery bag.

♂ **Your wife's purse**. Never carry it. If you have to (e.g. in the case of an emergency) then carry it like a football. NEVER carry it by the strap. The same man-logic applies to a diaper bag.

♂ **Pullin' a bag on wheels by the handle**. You might as well wear high heels and prance. This is especially true for wheelie-equipped gym bags.

♂ **Gift bags**. You know what we're talkin' about...those colorful bags with handles and tissue paper. Never make one, never take one, and never carry one.

♂ **Carryin' books chest-high**. This just doesn't look right. Men should carry books low (below the waist). Palm the spine with the pages facin' down.

♂ **Baby stroller**. We know you love your baby but when you and the misses pick out a stroller, make sure it is brown, dark gray or green.

♂ **Euro baby carriers**. You know, those contraptions that strap your baby to your chest or back. You've got two arms, use one to carry your baby.

♂ **Diaper bag**. See "Your wife's purse."

♂ **Eco-friendly bag**. A reusable shoppin' bag looks too much like a purse. Don't go there.

♂ **Mini shoppin' carts**. These just don't look right.

♂ **Haulin' a book bag with both straps**. Rucksacks and Campin' gear OK, not book bags.

15. IN THE BATHROOM

Watch it; this one can get you in real trouble. Just ask Senator what's-his-name. You'll be safer if you stay away from these Bathroom Manfractions.

♂ **Improper urinal spacin'**.[23] Never, never, never stand

---

[23] Man-spacin' is an important concept that requires clarification. You should always maintain proper man-spacin' both in space and in time. An example of improper man-spacin' includes walkin' so close that you could be mistaken for holdin' hands. This concept also applies to temporal man-spacin' (timing is everything). Never leave your table at the bar or restaurant to go to the bathroom at the same time (or in close proximity) with another man. Also, never take action that could negatively alter the man-spacin' calculus. For example, you and two of your buddies are out eatin' at a restaurant in a booth. You're sittin' on one side of the booth and they are on the other side. Before you get up for any reason, you have to coordinate with the other two so one of them can temporarily move to the other side. You can't just let them sit together on the same side of the booth. We know it's complicated but it must be done. In short, always de-conflict the man-space.

next to another dude at the urinals. Leave at least one space between. More if they're open. If there are three and the two outside ones are taken, find a stall. Never pick the middle urinal. You're just askin' another dude to join you. No stalls available? Hold it in. For the love of God, it's simply not worth it.

○ **Lookin'**. It's not a contest. You don't need to compare. Look straight ahead.

○ **Touchin'**. Don't pat your buddy on the back. He's got his junk in his hand for cryin' out loud!

○ **Talkin'**. Whatever you have to say can wait until you're both out of the bathroom.

○ **Follow-up stall usage**. Don't go into a stall some other dude just came out of. Find another one. Do you really want to share butt heat with some guy?

○ **Door crack lookin'**. Find another way to tell if the stall is occupied.

○ **Stall infringement**. You and all your stuff need to stay in your stall. Do not cross the stall border. We don't care how wide our stance is.

○ _____
○ _____
○ _____
○ _____
○ _____
○ _____
○ _____
○ _____
○ _____
○ _____
○ _____
○ _____

♂ _____

♂ _____

♂ _____

16. IN THE BEDROOM

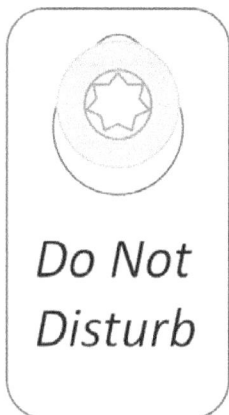

Do Not Disturb

Even though you may share your bedroom with your wife, you have to maintain some level of manliness. Say no to the followin':

♂ **Stuffed animals**. What are you...a little girl?
♂ **Extra pillows**. Remember that Ben Stiller movie "Along came Polly" where the wife of Ben Stiller's character had all those extra pillows? She cheated on him with their scuba instructor on their honeymoon. Those pillows are nothin' but trouble. Plus it's not practical. You have to take them off anyway to sleep.
♂ **Sayin' "I have a headache"**. Men do not have headaches in the bedroom. We are always willin' and able for that call to duty.
♂ _____
♂ _____
♂ _____
♂ _____
♂ _____

♂ _____

♂ _____

♂ _____

♂ _____

♂ _____

♂ _____

♂ _____

♂ _____

♂ _____

♂ _____

17. YOUR MUSIC

The kind of music you listen to says a lot about you as a man. Stay away from these and you'll be good to go.[24]

♂ **Elton John**. He's a walkin', singin', song writin', piano playin' Manfraction.

♂ **Barry Manilow**. "I write the songs..." that make me sound like a wimp. Perhaps we should call him Barry Manfractionilow.

♂ **Kenny G**. C'mon, he's blowin' on a long shaft. Do we have to spell it out for you?

♂ **Barbara Streisand**. We think that about covers it.

♂ **Bette Midler**. Right up there with Streisand.

♂ **The Village People**. Macho Man. YMCA, In the Navy...these titles sound cool right?...wrong, these "guys" had somethin' else in mind.

♂ **Michael Bolton**. If you listen to this guy, you might as well wear his concert T-Shirt or put up his poster in

---

[24] This section applies to listenin' to music on your radio or stereo as well as ring tones on your cell phone.

your bedroom. Man-up friend!

♂ **Madonna**.   As hot as she might be (or might have been)...too many fans on the other side of the plate, if you know what we mean.

♂ **Cher**. Whoa! Are you serious?

♂ **Show tunes**.   Broadway musicals?   You were in the choir in High School, weren't you?

♂ **Enya**. "Orinoco Flow?" What the hell is that?!

♂ **Clay Aiken.**

♂ **Michael Buble'.** He's no Sinatra

♂ **Two Dudes Singin' a Duet**.

♂ _____

♂ _____

♂ _____

♂ _____

♂ _____

♂ _____

♂ _____

♂ _____

♂ _____

♂ _____

♂ _____

♂ _____

♂ _____

♂ _____

♂ _____

18. MEDIA SOURCES

Let's face it. We have thousands of choices when it comes to magazines, movies and TV shows. Just because we have choices doesn't mean we should explore our inner woman. Stick to the manly alternatives and avoid these:

Magazines
- ♂ **Cosmopolitan**.
- ♂ **O: The Oprah Magazine**.
- ♂ **Vogue**.
- ♂ **Ladies Home Journal**.
- ♂ **Better Homes and Gardens**.
- ♂ **Southern Living**.
- ♂ **Playgirl**. No explanation needed.
- ♂ **Woman's Day**.
- ♂ **Lucky**. A women's magazine dedicated to shoppin'.
- ♂ **Ms. Magazine**.
- ♂ **Redbook**.
- ♂ **Working Mother**.
- ♂ **Venus**.
- ♂ **New Woman Magazine**.
- ♂ **International Woman**.
- ♂ **Moxie Magazine**.
- ♂ **The Pink Fridge**.
- ♂ **Today's Woman**.
- ♂ _____
- ♂ _____
- ♂ _____
- ♂ _____
- ♂ _____
- ♂ _____

♂ _____
♂ _____
♂ _____
♂ _____
♂ _____
♂ _____
♂ _____
♂ _____
♂ _____

Movies & Videos[25]

♂ **The English Patient**. We don't care if it has some war scenes or if the dude gets his thumbs chopped off.

♂ **Terms of Endearment**. A very touching movie but you cannot risk cryin' in public.

♂ **Little Women**. The title alone should signal alarms in your head.

♂ **The Color Purple**.

♂ **Titanic**.

♂ **The Truth about Cats and Dogs**. The truth about this movie is that it is a chick flick.

♂ **Pretty Woman**. Pretty much a chick flick. Plus, we've all heard the rumors about Richard Gere.

♂ **La Cage Au Folles**. Or, for that matter, any other movie that requires a translator. The same applies to subtitles. Men go to the movies to watch and listen, not to read!

♂ **Kramer vs. Kramer**.

♂ **Mystic Pizza**.

♂ **Shakespeare in Love**.

---

[25] It <u>may</u> be acceptable to go to a chick flick with your lady if you're confident it'll earn you some "alone time" later.

♂ **Sleepless in Seattle**.
♂ **Steel Magnolias**.
♂ **Chocolat**.
♂ **A Walk in the Clouds**.
♂ **A Walk to Remember**.
♂ **Brokeback Mountain**.
♂ **Thelma & Louise**.
♂ **Richard Simmons Exercise Videos**.
♂ **P.S. I Love You.**
♂ _____
♂ _____
♂ _____
♂ _____
♂ _____
♂ _____
♂ _____
♂ _____
♂ _____
♂ _____
♂ _____
♂ _____
♂ _____
♂ _____
♂ _____

TV Shows

♂ **Gardening shows**.   Unless there are tractors and hundreds of acres involved, flip the channel.
♂ **Sewing shows**.   Fabrics, little needles, crafts...who needs it?
♂ **Arts and crafts shows**. What? You gonna buy a little "Welcome to the Smith's. Est. 1999" plaque for the

front door?

♂ **Oxygen network**.   One exception…that elderly lady's sex show is OK. She's got some great ideas on how to make momma happy.

♂ **Oprah**.   Just a bunch of cryin', man-hatin', whiny women on there.

♂ **The View**. Ditto

♂ **Ellen**. Ditto

♂ **Designing Women**.

♂ **Golden Girls**.

♂ **Mad About You**.

♂ **Lifetime Channel**. Nothin' but a whole lot of women done wrong by men.

♂ **Anything on Bravo**.

♂ _____

♂ _____

♂ _____

♂ _____

♂ _____

♂ _____

♂ _____

♂ _____

♂ _____

♂ _____

♂ _____

♂ _____

♂ _____

♂ _____

♂ _____

19. GROOMIN'

Men should do as little grooming as possible. A real man doesn't really care how he looks. And as long as he doesn't smell like a dang horse, he's okay. Here are some things you should never do.

♂ **Primpin'**. Don't check yourself in the mirror. Don't fix your hair. Just leave it.[26]

♂ **Lotion**. You know what this stuff looks like. Why would you want to rub it on your body?

♂ **Brush**. Get a comb, sister.

♂ **Spendin' too much time gettin' ready**. If it takes you more than about 15 minutes, you're doin' somethin' wrong.

♂ **Salons**. Men go to barber shops. You know, those places with the red and white spiral signs and the men's magazines (we think they cut hair there too).

♂ **Loofas**. You need to keep those extra foliates. Like your back hair, you never know when it may come in handy.

♂ **Shower poofs**. You know, the little powder-puff of lacy fabric that hang in the shower. These things are clearly Manfractions.

♂ **Face mask with cucumber eye covers**. Please!

♂ **Exfoliators**. It's skin...who cares? Leave those foliates alone.

---

[26] Former U.S. Senator John Edwards was caught committin' a horrific Manfraction when a tape of him excessively primpin' himself before an interview made it to YouTube. Check it out – Google it. And to think, this guy was hopin' to be America's next President? No freakin' way!

♂ **Lip Balm** or **Lip Gloss**. Here's the deal – it looks like you're puttin' on lipstick.

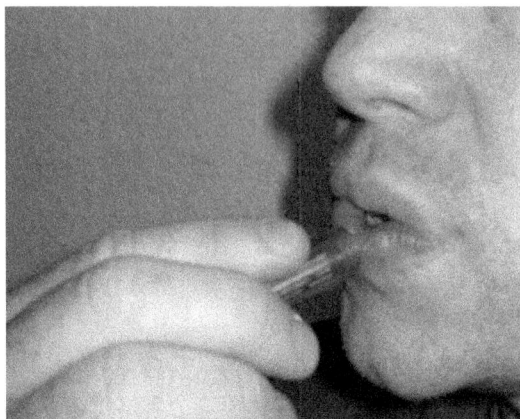

♂ **Cologne**. If you're puttin' on some "smell good" to get a lady, go for it. If you're goin' to work, the gym or to a game, forget it.[27]

♂ **Facials**. No man should ever get a facial, if you know what we mean.

♂ **Blow dryers**. You are wastin' valuable time! Use a towel and get on with your day.

♂ **Waxin'**. There is a reason you are hairy. Don't mess with Mother Nature.

♂ **Tannin' booths**. What if your buddies find out? A farmer's tan is better than a manufactured tan. Don't even think about a spray-on tan.

♂ **Eyebrow tweezin'**. It's not worth the extra effort or discomfort.

---

[27] Aqua Velva, Hai Karate, Brut and Lectric Shave remain acceptable. Splash it on – no spray pump involved!

Misc.

Just because some Manfractions defy categorization doesn't mean we should neglect to mention them. We list them here for your benefit:

♂ **Two men sittin' on a loveseat**. There is no love seat big enough for two men. The name alone implies somethin' you do not want to share with a man.

♂ **Usin' a watering can**. If you have to water the plants use a hose or hire the neighbor kid.

⚤ **Buyin' a man a gift card from certain stores**. Be careful. You may be abettin' a Manfraction. Your buddy may use it to buy Birkenstocks. Get him a card from a home improvement store or Sportin' goods store (or any other place on our "Absolution" list).

⚤ **Buyin' a birthday present for another man**. Generally speakin', you should not be runnin' out to buy gifts for another dude. If you have to you should not wrap it up with paper and ribbon. Acceptable "gifts" include buyin' a pitcher of beer or a lap dance.

⚤ **Buyin' flowers for a man**. Only if he's dead.

⚤ **Two or more men sharin' the same section of a revolving door**. This is a clear violation of man-spacin'.

⚤ **Usin' the metric system**. Don't describe the distance to the liquor store in kilometers. Don't tell people you weigh 90 kilograms.

⚤ **Headset cell phone**. What are you, Janet Jackson? You look like you're talkin' to yourself and it's freakin' us out. For the love of God, please stop.

⚤ **Colorful technology gizmos**. Your stuff should be white, black, or gray. Anythin' else and you're accessorizin'. Under no circumstances should you coordinate your tech gear (e.g. matchin' your music player with your cell phone or your gym outfit).

⚤ **Carryin' a balloon**. Unless you bought them for your wife or kids, you cannot do this.

⚤ **Changin' the channel away from sports**. Once you found the game on TV there is no need to go any further. We don't care how much you like American Idol, keep the channel on the ballgame. This act is compounded if you're out at Sport's Bar.

⚤ **Insufficient sports IQ**. Men must be proficient in the

language of sports. Next to food, women and beer, this is what men talk about most. This basic knowledge includes knowin' which team is the current reignin' champion (Super Bowl, World Series, NBA Championship, Nextel Cup, etc.). It also includes workin' knowledge of the basic sports rules. For example, you need to know about travellin' in basketball and the fact you run counterclockwise around the bases in baseball. You also have to know the current team names (e.g. it's the Baltimore Ravens, not the Baltimore Colts). Bottom line: If they're questionin' your fan-hood they're questionin' your manhood.

♂ **Havin' multiple "favorite" teams**. You should pick a team and stick with them until you die. The only exception to this is sayin' my favorite team is X and whoever is playin' Y. In this case you have a team you love (X) and a team you hate (Y). It's always OK to root for a team other than your favorite if you're hopin' the team you hate loses.

♂ **Improper gear**. For example, if you're playin' softball, you better not be wearin' runnin' shoes.

♂ **Posin' for a photo**. If you have to take a photo (e.g. yearbook, employee of the month, etc.) just take it. No restin' your hands by your face. No props. You should never get comfortable or flashy in front of the camera.

♂ **Usin' flower pens**. In an effort to keep folks from walkin' away with pens, places like banks and doctor's offices are makin' their collection of pens looks like an arrangement of flowers. Sometimes it's pretty hard to even tell they are pens. Keep it that way fellas. Don't fall into the trap of pluckin' one of these things an signin' a document with it. You know the tellers and receptionists are secretly laughin' at you. Plus, this Manfraction is likely bein' videotaped via the near-by security system. Bottom line: bring your own pen or ask for a real one.

⚣ **The Olympics**.

- o <u>Skin tight swimwear</u>. As mentioned earlier, these things are a bad idea. The ones they unveiled at the Beijing Games in 2008 were shockingly inappropriate. Heck, you couldn't tell the guys from the gals. We don't care if it's the latest technology...it's a Manfraction!

- o <u>Swim caps</u>. Shave your melon if you want to win the gold in a manly fashion!

- o <u>Shavin' below the neckline</u>. Armpits, chest, legs, etc.

- o <u>Badminton</u>. Shuttlecocks?! Real sports have balls.

- o <u>Speed-walkin'</u>. This is much harder than you think but there's way too much wigglin' goin' on.

- o <u>Holdin' flowers on the medal stand</u>. Hey, give the gold medal winner a beer!

- o <u>The 2-man Luge</u>. How can these "guys" live with themselves?

⚣ **Designin' or marketing a fragrance for men**. Think about it, you're puttin' your name on a product to make other men smell pretty.

⚣ **Buyin' a celebrity's fragrance for men**. Embrace your own natural man-scent, don't hide it. However, remember that for a night out with your special lady

Brut, Hai Karate and Lectric Shave are acceptable. What man wants to smell like Antonio Banderas or Tim McGraw?!

♂ **Overly enthusiastic worship**. It's OK for a man to have a relationship with God. However, public displays that include swayin', singin', and the clappin' of hands with eyes closed cross the line.

♂ **Cell phone charms**. A little too dainty, don't ya think?

♂ **Lettin' a chick decorate your man cave**. Dude, you've come so far by gettin' that man cave, don't blow it by lettin' her fill it with flowery curtains and doilies.

♂ **Bein' too "Green."** It's OK to save aluminum cans to raise some extra cash but don't go overboard. If you find yourself worryin' about the extra electricity used by your beer fridge, you've gone too far.

♂ **The MEN-gagement Ring**. This is a new trend out there where both men and women buy each other engagement rings. There's somethin' to be said for tradition.

♂ _____

♂ _____

♂ _____

♂ _____

♂ _____

♂ _____

♂ _____

♂ _____

♂ _____

♂ _____

♂ _____

♂ _____

♂ _____

ABSOLUTION

Okay, you've been through the book. You've pointed at all your buddies and laughed about how many Manfractions they've committed. But deep down, you know you committed a few yourself. Let's admit it, you feel a little dirty and ashamed. What do you do now? How does a man cleanse himself of the Manfraction grime that has accumulated? How can he regain that full sense of "Man" that he's lost? Let's take a look at some of the things you can do to renew and get your manhood back.

👍 **Go to a huge sportin' goods store**. These places are cool and we don't care if you have to drive a couple of hours to get to one. Consider it a pilgrimage. Walk around for at least an hour. Breathe deeply and take it all in. Test out some equipment. Buy some stuff. No, you're not shoppin', you're lettin' all the manliness of the place drive out the wimpiness that you've allowed to creep in.

👍 **Go on a big huntin'/fishin'/campin' trip**. Whatever your bag, you've got to get out there. No women, no phones, no TV (unless it's tuned to a 24-hour sports channel or a ballgame). Let the outdoors wash away all your transgressions. Kill somethin', or at least build a big fire. You'll get extra credit if you do this in cold temperatures (e.g. in the snow). Stare at the fire and poke it with a stick. Build a fire so powerful that you don't need to use a match to start it the next mornin'. Grunt a lot. Spit. Take a leak in the woods. You'll feel manlier in no time.

👍 **Do some adventure sports**. Kayakin', skydivin',

bungee jumpin', you name it. As long as you get the adrenaline pumpin' and it involves potential bodily harm. The danger factor will far overcome any accumulations of unmanliness.

- **Go to a ballgame**. Any level (pro to amateur) or any venue (indoor or outdoor). Get bonus man-points for attendin' a playoff game. The simple act of attendin' a sportin' event produces the right kind of chemicals and reconnects the right kind of neurons. Trust us here. You can't argue with science!

- **Eat chicken wings and drink beer**. Go to one of those sports bars with scantily clad young ladies. Those places were designed for the man.

- **Buy a really nice grill**. Precision outdoor cookin'. It doesn't get any better! Get a big slab of meat and let your manly masterpiece do the rest.

- **Read a men's magazine cover to cover**. Read? Yeah, right.

- **Attend a Rodeo or bull ridin' event**. With all that testosterone flyin' around, you're bound to get some on ya'. You'll forget about that man-bag carryin' episode in no-time.

- **Watch sports shows on cable TV**. These days there are more and more of these kinds of shows and that's good! You'll see clips and outtakes from the world of sports, the latest scores and highlights and behind the scenes access to your favorite teams. When you're a better fan, you're a better man.

- **Go to a big hardware store and buy some lumber and tools**. Like the big sportin' goods stores, hardware or home improvement stores can be cathartic. There are so many tools, and so much to learn. It's a very humbling experience.

👍 **Make yourself a sloppy joe sandwich**. The name says it all. If you're not makin' a mess, you're not gettin' the full experience.

👍 **Get a big ol' fast food burger**. Don't worry if you get a little ketchup or burger juice on your shirt.

👍 **Fix somethin' with duct tape**. You should never be without this stuff. Keep some in your car. Keep a roll in the garage. Pack it in your survival kit. You never know what you might have to fix.

👍 **Clean your man cave or your garage with a heavy duty shop vacuum.** Wet or Dry.

👍 **Buy and install one of those big sports decals**. Nothin' says you wear the pants in the family like a life-sized poster of Brian Urlacher in your livin' room.

👍 **Buy yourself a road-worthy motorcycle**. Nothin' reeks manhood like a motorcycle. Don't forget the leather jacket (no sequins please).

👍 **Visit a sports restaurant / bar**. There are some very impressive ones out there with all the creature comforts. We're talkin' surround sound, huge high definition TVs and lounge chairs. Some even have TVs in the bathrooms so you never miss a play.

👍 **Portable urinal**. Speakin' of never missin' a play, there are devices out there that can make that happen. Nothin' speaks to your commitment to beer and the game like this brilliant piece of men-gineering.

👍 **Go to professional auto racin' event**. Better yet, camp out the night before and the night after. Tip: Bring some beads for the ladies.

👍 **Go to an "all you can eat" buffet**. Don't be shy...make it an all day event.

👍 **Equip your ride at an auto parts store**. Batteries, brake fluid, tires...these places have it all!

👍 **Watch shows catered to the man**. Get ideas on how to trick out your man cave. Do fake breasts sink or float? Sometimes "girls jumpin' on trampolines" is just what the doctor ordered.

👍 _____

👍 _____

👍 _____

👍 _____

👍 _____

👍 _____

👍 _____

👍 _____

👍 _____

👍 _____

👍 _____

👍 _____

👍 _____

👍 _____

👍 _____

MANFRACTION SCENARIO TEST

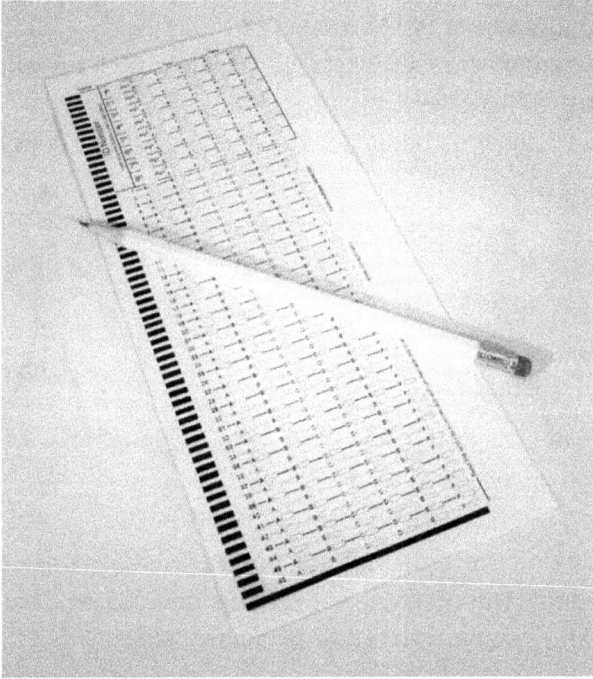

Now that you've reached the end of this book it's time to see what you've learned. Take the followin' scenario-based test to see how good you are at detectin' and avoidin' Manfractions. You can take an extended version of this test on Manfraction.com. Remember how we said Manfractions are not always cut and dried? You'll see that in this test. Pick the best answer.

1. Nature calls and you head to the men's room. Four urinals with dudes usin' the two end ones. You:

a. proudly use urinal number two.
b. ask one of the two pissin' gents when he'll be finished.
c. use a stall.
d. cry to momma because you're about to pee your pants.

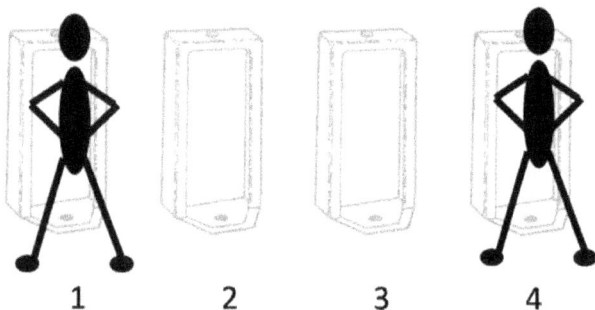

1   2   3   4

2. Makin' momma happy, you're walkin' through the local department store when she decides to "try these on." She asks you to hold her purse. You:

a. flatly refuse because you're a man.
b. take the purse and put it on the floor as you wait.
c. take the purse and hold it in your lap while you wait
d. take the purse and swing it from your hand as you look at some stunning tops.

3. You're at the movies watchin' Titanic when your boss spots you and then proceeds to sit in the empty seat right next to. You:

a. hug your boss and thank him for carin' enough to sit with you.

b. leave the theater without sayin' a word.

c. get up and move one seat over so there is one seat between the two of you.

d. invite your boss to a sports bar to absolve the fact you went to a chick flick by yourself.

4. You wake up one mornin' to discover your wife has taken your car and left you her mini Euro-car. She has a vanity plate that says SHOEFRK, a crystal danglin' from the mirror and a bumper sticker that says "Maneater." You work at a sawmill 20 miles from your house. You:

a. walk the 20 miles to work.

b. drive your wife's car to work.

c. sell your wife's car to the first person stupid enough to buy it.

d. rip off the plates, tear the crystal down, scrape off the bumper sticker, then drive her bug.

5. You're at the local pub. You order a beer. The waitress asks if you want lime/lemon/orange with that. You:

a. say yes, that sounds yummy.
b. say "no, that would be a Manfraction."
c. look around to see if your buddies are listenin' and ask her to push it down in the bottle so no one will notice.
d. say no, but how about a spritz of soda water.

6. You and your wife are expectin' your first baby and you find out it's gonna be a boy. Your wife wants to name your son after her late Aunt Leslie who raised her and was an all around great woman. You:

a. agree to name your heir Leslie because you're makin' momma happy.
b. agree because Leslie Nielson is one of your favorite actors.
c. disagree because men should not be named after chicks.
d. disagree because men should not have unisex names.
e. both c and d.

7. You're at a wedding reception (open bar) when a waitress hands you a cocktail. You:

a. drink up because it's alcohol and it's free!
b. remove the lemon and enjoy it.
c. remove the umbrella and drink away.
d. say "no thanks, I'll have a beer."
e. both b and c.

8. Your wife bought you some tassel shoes for Christmas and wants you to wear them to work. What do you do?

a. say "yes dear," and wear the shoes to work.
b. forget her and wear your old shoes.
c. wear the tassel shoes out the door but change into your old shoes in the car on the way to work.
d. wear the charm-covered rubber shoes you bought yourself for Christmas instead.

9. You just finished workin' out and it's time to hit the showers before you head back to the office. There are five showers available, with the two end showers occupied. You:

a. enter without fanfare and use shower #3 .
b. slide right in there to shower #2 and lather up.
c. enter and ask the guy in shower #5 if it's OK to use shower #3.
d. wait to enter until one of the two guys leaves and take the unoccupied end spot.

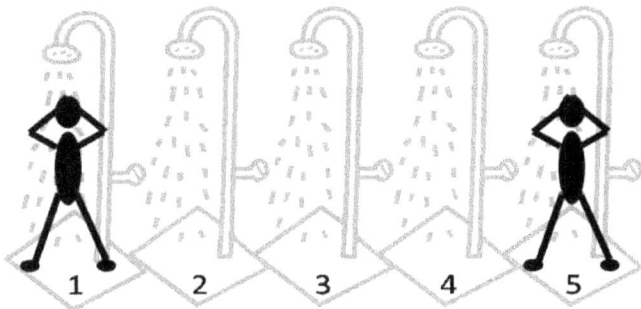

10.   When you're finished takin' a shower you realize you forgot your towel. You:

a. Ask your buddy to borrow his towel.
b. Ask a stranger to borrow his towel.
c. Dry off with your workout shirt.
d. Go naked into the sauna to dry off.

MANFRACTION SCENARIO TEST ANSWERS

1. c.

- "a" is wrong because you shouldn't piss next to another guy.
- "b" is wrong because you shouldn't talk to another guy while he's pissin'.
- "d" is wrong because cryin' to momma is never an excuse when you're a man.

2. b

- "a" is wrong because flat out refusin' to do somethin' is not the best way to make momma happy.
- "c" is wrong because you should not hold a purse.
- "d" is wrong because you're bein' way too comfortable with that purse.

3. d

- "a" is wrong because men don't hug
- "b" is not the best answer. Pretendin' the Manfraction did not occur is not an appropriate response. When you're called out you take it like a man – no whinin' no quibblin'
- "c" is not the best answer. Although you should be commended for attemptin' to maintain the proper man-spacin' you need to realize that are invitin' another dude to watch a chick flick with you.

4. a.

- "b" is wrong not only because it is a min-car, but because of the plates, crystal and bumper sticker.
- "c" is not the best answer. Dude, your wife would kill you if you sold her car. Self-Preservation and Makin' Momma happy both apply here!
- "d" is not the best answer. It's too late to take such drastic actions. The next time you should negotiate with your wife to make her car more gender neutral in case of emergencies.

5. b.

- "a" is wrong because men should not put fruit in their beer and they should not say "yummy."
- "c" is wrong because you're still committin' a Manfraction. Deception is not the answer.
- "d" is wrong because men should not say "spritz."

6. e (both c and d).

- "a" is wrong because this is too much ground to give to please Momma. Names are permanent and require lots of time and money to change them.
- "b" is wrong. With all due respect to Mr. Nielson, he's got a chick's name.
- "c" is not the best answer. With all due respect to Aunt Leslie, you should not name your son after her.
- "d" is not the best answer. It is true that men should not have unisex names but in this case that is not the whole story (see above).

7. d.

- "a" is wrong because you'd be acceptin' a fancy-ass cocktail.
- "b" is wrong because after removin' the lemon, there's still an umbrella in your drink.
- "c" is wrong because after removin' the umbrella, there's still a lemon in your drink.
- "e" is wrong because you'd still be acceptin' a cocktail.

8. c.

- "a" is wrong because men should not wear shoes with tassels.
- "b" is wrong because you need to be nice to and show some respect to Momma.
- "d" is wrong because rubber shoes with charms are a compound Manfraction.

9. a.

- "b" is wrong because you should not stand right next to a naked man.
- "c" is wrong because you should not talk to a naked man.
- "d" is not the best answer. You can accomplish your mission (takin' a quick shower so you can get back to work) and still maintain proper man-spacin' by usin' shower #3.

10. c.

- "a" is wrong because you should not share your buddy's body moisture.
- "b" is wrong because you should not share a stranger's body moisture.
- "d" is wrong because you'd have to walk around in the buff and bare ass the bench.

APPENDIX – THE CALL SIGN NAMIN' CEREMONY

There's a tradition in the military that is worthy of mention in this book. The namin' ceremony. You'll remember our earlier section on how "Your Name" can be a Manfraction. The namin' ceremony is a way to get a new one. The call sign developed in response to the need to identify fighter pilots over the radio in a concise manner. Now you and your buddies can get call signs to get rid of those pansy-ass names you have.

To get a call sign you'll need the followin': Your buddies, beer, and a white board. Your buddies will already have a few names they think are appropriate. They'll write these possible call signs down on the white board. You then let your buddies know what you'd like your call sign to by tellin' a story. The story should be humorous and preferably racy, but doesn't necessarily have to be completely true. Follow the "10% rule." 10% of your story should be true. Be careful though, because many other potential call signs will emerge as you tell your story. A scribe jots down these other potential additional names on the white board durin' the story and one of these could become your call sign. For example, one of our buddies wanted a certain nickname but became known as "Archie" because his story contained a bit about him streakin' under the St. Louis Arch.

Put some thought into your story…the funnier and more unbelievable the better. For instance, if you want your call sign to be Tex and you tell a story about how you're from Texas and you graduated from college in Texas and you

135

really like Texas, chances are your buddies will give you a call sign like "Ass Man." But if you tell a story about how you went to a Cowboys' game and afterward all the cheerleaders came over to your place and you had them all screamin', "Tex, oh Tex!", you might just end up as Tex from then on. After your story, you leave the room so the rest of the group can deliberate. When they've decided they'll let you back in and tell you what you're now called.

You can live with this new call sign, or you can challenge this name via a re-attack later. Be warned, a re-attack will require another (hopefully better) story, and lots of bribes and offerin's.

Remember, you don't have to be stuck with a wimpy name, have a namin' ceremony and get a call sign. We'd love to hear some of the great stories and call signs you guys come up with. Put 'em on Manfraction.com today.

ABOUT THE AUTHORS

Doug "36" Drake is a former US Army Green Beret. If he told us about the missions he's been on, he'd have to kill us. When he's not grillin' dead animals, you'll find him skydivin' or ridin' his Harley.

Scott "Blue" Maethner is a Minnesota native and prefers sub-zero temperatures. Despite havin' three young kids, he's never owned a minivan. He likes football, power tools and drinkin' beer.

Derek "Gees" Geeskie is a proud Hoosier who is at home with a cold homebrew and a bag of chips while watchin' hoops. He spends his weekends target shootin' and boiling down the finest hops.

www.ingramcontent.com/pod-product-compliance
Lightning Source LLC
LaVergne TN
LVHW021508080426
835509LV00018B/2436